Remission Impossible

Rabbi Yonatan Emmett

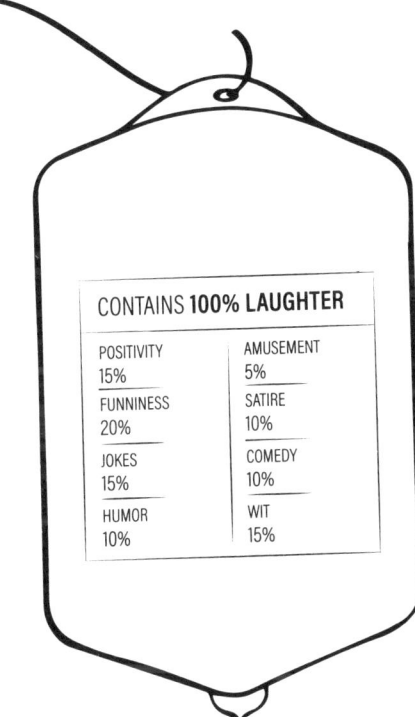

CONTAINS 100% LAUGHTER

POSITIVITY 15%	AMUSEMENT 5%
FUNNINESS 20%	SATIRE 10%
JOKES 15%	COMEDY 10%
HUMOR 10%	WIT 15%

Remission Impossible

A CANCER PATIENT'S SERIOUSLY FUNNY GUIDE TO LIFE

Mosaica Press, *with its team of acclaimed editors and designers, is attracting some of the most compelling thinkers and teachers in the Jewish community today. Our books are impacting and engaging readers from around the world.*

Copyright © 2024 by Mosaica Press

All rights reserved. No part of this book may be used or reproduced or transmitted in any form or by any means, electronic or mechanical, including photocopying, recording, or by any information storage and retrieval system, without written permission from the publisher.

ISBN: 978-1-961602-68-7

Published by Mosaica Press, Inc.
www.mosaicapress.com
info@mosaicapress.com

Dedication

Dedicated in loving memory to

Happiness

You are dearly missed.

Apologies

To my British readers—I apologize
for using American spelling.
Feel free to insert these at random: u u u u u u

To my American readers—my apologies
for my use of British vocabulary.
Without the word "rubbish,"
this book would be incomplete.

To my non-English-speaking readers—
how are you reading this?

Acknowledgments

This book has been made possible
thanks to paper, and cancer.

Disclaimer

All identifying details, names, and places
have been omitted from this work.
This was not done in order to protect anyone's privacy,
but because why in the world would anyone be interested
in the biographical details of someone who isn't famous yet?

Warning

This book may contain traces of humor.
Side effects include mild amusement,
a general sense of well-being,
and uncontrollable bursts of laughter.
Read in public at your own peril.

מוסדות אור שמח מרכז טננבאום ע.ר. 58-00-21343-00
רח׳ שמעון הצדיק 22-28 ירושלים ת.ד. 18103
טל: 02-581-0315

Michtav Bracha
Adar 1, 5784

Dear R' Yonatan,

Thank you for letting me see your book. It is not the typical *chizuk-emunah-bitachon* type of treatment, but in its very unique way can and will provide genuine *chizuk* for people in distress and for the families trying to support them.

First, your book is real. You openly talk about nausea, vomiting, loss of hair, loss of appetite, weakness. This is important; you are not sugarcoating an unpleasant reality. You are honest; the reader knows you are telling it as it is. The reader knows you have been through, and are going through, all of this. Honesty gives you credibility. You know of what you speak.

Second, attitude matters. Looking at the adversities of life with humor gives you the strength to deal with them. It gives you the ability to continue to have a meaningful, productive life even with illness. This is an extraordinarily important message.

I endorse and support what you are doing as well as the unconventional way you are doing it. The religious messages of *bitachon, hashgacha, kabbolas yisurin b'ahava* are not necessarily explicit but they are definitely there between the lines, and like the proverbial spoonful of sugar that makes the medicine go down, your humor and wit will enable people to absorb the spiritual lessons you are conveying. The great physicist Niels Bohr (Jewish but not observant) once remarked, "There are some things so serious that you have to laugh at them." There is great wisdom in his words.

After reading your chapter on inappropriate things to say, I am a bit tongue-tied as to what I should wish you, but I believe I can say that Hashem should give you *arichus yamim* with a minimum of pain and suffering and with the ability to learn and teach Torah and to enjoy your life with your wife and children.

With admiration and bracha,
Yitzchak A. Breitowitz
Rav, Kehillat Ohr Somayach

Rabbi Edward Reichman, MD

As a historian of medicine, I am aware of the ancient Hippocratic theory of the four "humors." While this was abandoned centuries ago, it appears Rabbi Emmett has reformulated it into the theory of the one "humor." The therapeutic effects of laughter and humor have long been anecdotally known, but Rabbi Emmett's comedic masterpiece takes the adage "laughter is the best medicine" to an entirely new level. In a world of remarkable new advances in cancer treatment, Rabbi Emmett, a master Torah educator, incorporates his personal experience battling cancer to create a genuinely new modality in cancer therapy.

Inspirational is simply not descriptive enough to capture the experience of reading this book. It successfully explores the gamut of human emotions created by living a life with cancer, making them accessible, relatable, and humorous.

You will laugh about cancer and not only not feel guilty about it—it will be liberating and exhilarating. Yes, it is brilliantly witty and clever, and masterfully written, but its value goes far beyond the words on the page. It will not only gladden your heart, but your lungs, liver, and kidneys as well. It is a healing balm for body and soul. I am confident that a controlled scientific study will verify the therapeutic effects of this work, and I would highly recommend that you enroll in the clinical trials immediately. It is the only cancer therapy in the world that has no untoward side effects (though you might get some pains from excessive laughter). God willing, the author himself, and all those suffering from cancer, will greatly benefit from this novel therapy for years to come.

Rabbi Edward Reichman, MD
Professor, Emergency Medicine,
Albert Einstein College of Medicine
Isaac and Bella Tendler Chair
of Jewish Medical Ethics, Yeshiva University

Hanoch Teller

Norman Cousins move over, for the first time in forever, Rabbi Yonatan Emmett has truly mastered the powerful drug of laughter. We are talking a Normandy Invasion of side-splitting humor.

It takes quite an intellect to see the funny side of cancer, but as Rabbi Sinai Adler responded when asked, "How could a Holocaust survivor smile so much?" he replied, "What is my other option?"

Although my personal medical knowledge is abysmal, I think we all understand that an optimistic patient, open to humor, handles the vagaries of illness better than one who is depressed and defeatist. Despair is never in the patient's interest and Rabbi Emmett has harnessed an interminable arsenal of witty and laugh-out-loud antidepressants as he leads the reader along his journey of diagnosis and coping with cancer. Vindication of Nehru's quip, "Life is like a game of cards. The hand that is dealt to you represents determinism, the way you play it is free will."

Ultimately, Rabbi Emmett—who never lets on where he is going, and with his superb comic timing—up against pain, hospital tedium, endless annoyances, and a nefarious disease, has the last laugh. Read *Remission Impossible* as a sure-fire Rx for far more minor-league problems.

Hanoch Teller

Professor Aaron Ciechanover, MD, DSc

בספרו Remission Impossible מעלה יהונתן אמת הרהורים כנים, אך בעיקר הגיגים הומוריסטיים, של חולה סרטן המסרב לקחת את החיים ברצינות. יהונתן חלה בממאירות של הדם הקרויה מיאלומה נפוצה בה מתרבה תא בודד של המערכת החיסונית בקצב מהיר ותופס את מקומו של כל חלל מח העצם, הלא הוא המפעל המייצר את כל כדוריות הדם. זכורני, כסטודנט לרפואה בשנות ה־60 וה־70, כי החולים נפטרו מן המחלה בסבל רב תוך שנה או שנתיים מיום אבחנתה. בסוף שנות ה־90 חל מהפך של ממש בטיפול במחלה. תגלית ישראלית של מערכת תאית לבקרת איכות של חלבונים (שזיכתה את מגליה—הפרופסורים אברהם הרשקו ואהרן צ'חנובר, כותב דברים אלו, בפרס נובל לכימיה לשנת 2004) הביאה לפיתוח סדרת תרופות ששינו באופן קיצוני את תמונת המחלה. התרופות מאריכות את חיי חלק גדול מהחולים לעשור ויותר, חלקם נרפאים מן המחלה, וחשוב ביותר, הם חיים כאנשים בריאים באיכות חיים מצוינת. מדובר במהפכה של ממש. יהונתן נמנה על חולים אלו.

נחזור אבל לסיפורו האישי ולספרו. רוב האנשים המאובחנים במחלות שתג הממאירות מתנוסס מעליהן, שוקעים במרה שחורה, וחייהם וחיי משפחותיהם מתחילים לסוב סביב המחלה. יהונתן אמר לעצמו מן הסתם שבמילא גורלו מופקד בידי התרופות, הרופאים הטובים, אבל גם, ואולי במידה רבה, בידי התייחסותו שלו אל המחלה. הוא התייחס אליה לכן בהומור, כמעין חבר חדש לחיים, שכן חדש שלא הוא בחר בו ואשר נכנס לפתע לחייו, אבל שכדאי לחיות עמו מן הסתם בקלילות. וכי מדוע לריב? הוא והשכן מתמידים ביחסיהם הטובים עד עצם היום הזה, כשהשכן נעלם מעט לעת—מה שידוע בעגה הרפואית כמנוחה מן המחלה (remission), חוזר לעתים, אך נעלם לו שוב. ובינתיים חלפו שנים, יהונתן חי בריא בחיק חבריו ומשפחתו, לא מעט בשל נפשו הבריאה החבויה בגופו הבריא. לוואי וחולים רבים היו מאמצים גישה הומוריסטית זו שללא ספק תפקיד חשוב לה בשיפור חיים ובהחלמה מחוליים רבים.

אהרן צ'חנובר
חתן פרס נובל לכימיה לשנת 2004

Professor Aaron Ciechanover, MD, DSc

In his book *Remission Impossible*, Yonatan Emmett shares the honest reflections, but mostly the humorous musings, of a cancer patient who refuses to take life seriously. Yonatan has a type of blood cancer called multiple myeloma, in which a single cell of the immune system multiplies at a rapid rate and fills the entire cavity that houses the bone marrow, the factory that produces all blood cells. I remember, as a medical student in the 1960s and 1970s, that patients with multiple myeloma would die from the disease with great suffering within a year or two from the time of its diagnosis. At the end of the 1990s, there was a transformation in the treatment of the disease. The Israeli discovery of a cellular system for quality control of proteins (that won its finders, Professors Avraham Hershko and Aharon Ciechanover, writer of these words, the Nobel Prize in Chemistry for 2004) led to the development of a series of drugs that radically changed the face of the disease. These drugs prolong the lives of a large number of the patients for a decade or more, some of them are cured of the disease, and most importantly, they live as healthy people with an excellent quality of life. This was a real revolution. Yonatan is one of these patients.

To return to Yonatan's personal story and his book, many people who are diagnosed with diseases that are labeled as malignant sink into melancholy, and their lives and the lives of their families begin to revolve around the disease. Yonatan probably told himself that his fate was in the hands of the medicines, the good doctors, but also, and perhaps to a great extent, in the hands of his own attitude towards the disease. He therefore treated it with humor, as a kind of new friend for life, a new neighbor that he did not choose and who suddenly entered his life, but with whom it is probably worth living cordially. And why fight? He and the neighbor persist in their good relationship to this very day, with the neighbor disappearing from time to time—what is known in medical parlance as a remission from the disease, returning sometimes, and disappearing again.

And in the meantime, years have passed, Yonatan lives healthily in the comfort of his friends and family, in no small part due to the healthy spirit hidden in his healthy body. I highly recommend that other patients adopt this humorous approach, which undoubtedly plays a significant role in improving life and recovering from many illnesses.

Aaron Ciechanover, MD, DSc
Laureate, 2004 Nobel Prize in Chemistry
Member (Foreign), USA National Academies
of Sciences (NAS) and Medicine (NAM)
The Rappaport Family Technion Integrated Cancer Center (R-TICC)
Honorary President of The Israel Cancer Association

Talmudic Encyclopedia Ins. Ltd. Pbc.   הוצאת אנציקלופדיה תלמודית בע"מ חל"צ

בס"ד, בחודש אדר ב, תשפ"ד

לכבוד הרב יהונתן אמת שליט"א,

קבלתי לנכון את ספרך היחיד והמיוחד המונח לפני הקוראים.

הספר מיועד לחולים במחלות ממאירות, הגורמות סבל מתמשך וקשה הן מעצם המחלה, הן מהטיפולים הקשים בה, והן מהצורך לקבל החלטות מורכבות וקשות במהלך הארוך והמייגע של המחלה.

אתה כותב את הספר המיוחד הזה מתוך ניסיון אישי בכל הצמתים הללו, וזה כמובן מוסיף נופך רב למסרים שבספר.

המיוחד בספרך הוא המבט ההומוריסטי והשנון על כל החוויות שחולה במחלות קשות כאלה עובר במשך תקופה ארוכה. הוא כתוב ברגישות רבה, מבלי לפגוע בשום אדם.

בטוחני שכל חולה במחלה קשה יפיק תועלת רבה וייחודית מספרך, אשר משרה אווירה אופטימית, יחד עם הבנה עמוקה במצב כמות שהוא, עקב כתיבתך השוטפת, החדה, השנונה וההומוריסטית.

במחלות קשות וכרוניות, הגורמות סבל וכאב רב, נהגים מאז ומעולם לטפל בתרופות, בניתוחים, ובמכשירים שונים בהתאם לאופי המחלה ולהתקדמותה.

אכן זו גישה לצד הפיזי של הבעיה.

מאידך, ידוע מקדמת דנא שהאדם מורכב גם מגוף וגם מנפש, גם מהצד הגופני-הגשמי וגם מהצד הפסיכולוגי-הרוחני, והמרכיב האחרון חשוב לא פחות מהמרכיב הראשון בהליך החלמתו והתמודדותו של חולה במחלה קשה. היינו, ככל שהאדם הסובל והכואב אופטימי יותר, שמח יותר, ומתעלה יותר באמונה ובתפילה—כך מתחזקים בו הכוחות הנחוצים להתמודד עם הבעיה הפיזית-גשמית.

ספרך—הן בתוכן והן בסגנון—מטפל בצורה ייחודית בהעלאת המורל, השמחה, האופטימיות והרוחניות של החולה, ובכך מהווה הוא תרומה משמעותית מאד בקידום בריאותו, הצלחת הטיפול הפיזי-גופני שלו, והצלחת החלמתו ממחלתו הקשה.

התועלת מספרך היא לא רק לחולה עצמו, אלא גם לבני משפחתו, לידידיו ולשוחרי טובתו. גם הם נתונים במתחים נפשיים ובהתמודדויות קשות נוכח המצב הקשה של יקירם. האתנחתא ההומוריסטית השנונה בקריאה בספרך—בוודאי תשפר את מצב רוחם, ותאפשר להם להתמודד טוב יותר עם המצב הקשה, ובכך לסייע טוב יותר לחולה הזקוק לעזרתם ולתמיכתם.

הנני מאחל לך בריאות שלמה ומלאה, המשך עשייה מבורכת, והצלחה בכל אשר תעשה.

אני ממליץ בחום לכל החולים במחלות קשות ולבני משפחותיהם ואוהביהם לקרוא את הספר הזה.

בברכה נאמנה,

הרב פרופ' אברהם שטינברג

רח' שמואל הנגיד 30 | ת.ד. 71111 | ירושלים | 9171002 | Jerusalem | P.O.B. 71111 | Sh'muel Hanagid Str.
טל' 02-6423242 | פקס' 02-6423821 | אתר web. talmudit.org | e-mail. office@e-tal.org | Fax. 972(0)2-6423821 | 972(0)2-6423242

Talmudic Encyclopedia Ins. Ltd. Pbc.   הוצאת אנציקלופדיה תלמודית בע"מ חל"צ

I have received your unique book that is hereby placed before the readers.

The book is intended for patients suffering from malignant diseases, which cause continuous and severe suffering, from the disease itself, the grueling treatments, and the need to make complex and difficult decisions during the long and tiring course of the illness.

You write this special book from your own experience at all these junctures, which, of course, gives a personal touch and adds value to the messages in the book.

The uniqueness of your book is in the humorous and witty view of all the experiences that patients with suchlike serious illnesses go through over a long period of time. It is written with great sensitivity, without offending anyone.

I am sure that every patient suffering from a serious illness will derive great and unique benefit from your book, which instills an optimistic atmosphere, together with a deep understanding of the situation as it is, due to your fluent, sharp, witty, and humorous writing.

In serious and chronic illnesses, which cause great suffering and pain, it has always been customary to treat with drugs, surgeries, and various devices, depending on the nature of the disease and its progress.

Indeed this is the approach to the physical side of the problem.

On the other hand, it has long been known that man consists of both a body and a soul, a physical-material side and a psychological-spiritual side, and the latter element is no less important than the former in the process of coping with and recovery from serious illness. In other words, when a patient is more optimistic, happy, and uplifted in his faith and prayer, the forces necessary to deal with the physical-material problem become stronger.

Your book—both in content and style—deals in a unique way with raising the morale, joy, optimism, and spirituality of the patient, and as such it makes a very significant contribution to promoting his health, the success of his physical treatment, and recovery from serious illness.

The benefit of your book is not only for the patient himself, but also for his family members, friends, and all who wish him well. They too are subject to mental stress and struggles due to the difficult condition of their loved one. The wit and humor of your book will surely provide them with a well-needed break and lift their spirits, thus enabling them to better deal with the challenging situation, in turn assisting the patient who needs their help and support.

I wish you full and complete health, continued productivity, and success in all your endeavors.

I highly recommend that all patients of serious illnesses and their families and loved ones read this book.

Sincerely,

Rabbi Professor Avraham Steinberg

Advance Praise

"In this unusual book, Yonatan Emmett achieves the seemingly impossible: showing how to deal with serious adversity through humor. This is a work that is both deep and funny. Anyone dealing with personal difficulties who reads it will be stimulated to see themselves and their ordeals through new eyes. A truly fresh perspective."

Rabbi Dr. Akiva Tatz

"It is a valuable skill to be able to cope well with health challenges. We all need a positive mental attitude and a healthy sense of humor to access the inner resources that are so important. The author has done a wonderful service for all who will gain from reading this book. It's an immense kindness."

Rabbi Zelig Pliskin
Author, Six Wonderful Habits for a Wonderful Life

"It's remarkable how rotten of a human you conclude you are when finding yourself laughing at someone's account of their cancer. Nonetheless, it is unavoidable in this case. Yonatan Emmett is a sharp observer of the human condition (especially his own), a witty, mordant, immensely likeable tour guide through one version of Hell, someone who you are rooting for intensely."

Professor Robert Sapolsky
Professor of Biology, Neurology, and Neurosurgery,
Stanford University

Table of Contents

Prologue... xxi
Another Prologue, Apparently xxiii

Part One

1	From So Simple a Beginning 3
2	Check-Room-Mate 9
3	The Cards We're Dealt 14
4	Food for Thought 18
5	Knock, Knock......................................23
6	Cry as You May 29
7	The Future of Mankind 34
8	Rhyme and Reason 42
9	No Such Luck......................................44
10	Taxi Returns......................................48
11	Take a Seat.......................................53
12	Leading the Poles 56
13	Hearty Donation 60
14	Pains and Needles 67
15	Healthy, Wealthy, and Happy Ever After 72
16	Impatient Inpatient 77

17	Ice, Ice Maybe..................................83
18	Unhappy Feet...................................89
19	A Better Pill to Swallow 92
20	Don't Be My Guest 95
21	Goodbye, Sweetie 98
22	Mask of Misery, Pillar of Pain 102
23	Hair Today, Gone Tomorrow 106
24	Crash Course 111
25	Sir Cancer Can 114
26	Outpatients and Inmates..........................115
27	Know Thy Place.................................117
28	Over the Hills and Far Away 120
29	What Makes You Tick?...........................124
30	Side-Burns 130
31	Driving the Point Home..........................136
32	Good Mourning.................................140
33	Save the Date...................................143
34	Looking Forward................................146

Part Two

35	The Show Must Go On. And On. And On............151
36	Survivors' Guild.................................153
37	Writing Has No Wry.............................157
38	Trial and Terror.................................163
39	A Bumpy Start..................................167

40	Side Notes 170
41	Learn and Live 173
42	Fishing for Complements 177
43	Respiratory Respite 183
44	Long Time No See 187
45	Read between the Lines 196
46	Man's Search for Gleaning 204
47	The Writing on the Wall 208
48	Wait Watchers 211
49	Two Strikes and You're In 214
50	Love of Labor 219
51	(Not) The Final Chapter 224

Acknowledgments 226

Prologue
The Good, the Bad, and the Really, Really Bad

Thou shalt not stop laughing.

Life

Cancer, alternatively known by its technical name, "that thing that happens to other people," is no laughing matter. Life, on the other hand—that thing that happens to all people—certainly is. Or, indeed, it should be if we are to stand a chance of surviving it.

Readers of this book may get the impression that my cancer experience has been, in some unnatural and miraculous way, not entirely unpleasant, perhaps even enjoyable, and—in some bizarre way—fun. Such an impression would be justified, considering the manner in which I chose to describe the events and my reactions to them. But it would be utterly false, immensely so. I experienced more than my fair share of hardships—intense nausea, relentless vomiting, crippling stomach cramps, extreme fatigue, frustrating insomnia, overwhelming weakness, high fever, throbbing bone aches, and a hundred other flavors of pain and misery.

And some lesser-known side effects, too. The trance like, steroid-fueled frenzies and their counterpart crashes deserve a chapter of their own, indeed a book of their own, indeed a universe of their own, in which they might resemble some form of bizarre normality; the absolute heartbreak, when finally, upon returning home after a month in isolation, I was not able to hug or kiss my children due to a deficient immune system; how on the following morning, I awoke to find that I had aged fifty years overnight and could not move any part of my body, my heart pounding and my breathing heavy from the effort of merely existing. And how can I forget the daily encounter with the pale, gaunt, bald, ghostly figure that appeared in my bathroom mirror every morning, somehow managing to shock me anew each time?

Such highlights, or lowlights to be accurate, were not in short stock. Their absence from this book, or at least the absence of a befitting description of their full impact, is not proof of their nonexistence, merely a reflection of the type of book I chose to write and the way in which I chose to write it. Our bookshelves are already groaning under the heavy load of volume upon volume packed with human suffering. And human courage and triumph, too. But, to the best of my knowledge, few are the shelves that sport a humorous illness book, by an author intent on outliving cancer and outlaughing life, no matter the circumstances. Such literary creatures are rare, if they even exist at all.

Or at least so I thought when I started writing this book. Then, upon mentioning my novel endeavor to an acquaintance, I was informed that someone else had already done something of the like. In fact, as time passed, I discovered that several such books existed, and that the phenomenon seemed to have taken on the form of a trend of sorts, something I passionately try to avoid. Indeed, I now fear that in no time at all, all books available in the market will strictly be cancer comedies, until one day in the far future, a brave author, willing to endure harsh literary criticism and ridicule, will dare write about the subject gravely once again, taking life, and himself, very seriously. One thing is certain, though — that author won't be me.

Another Prologue, Apparently
The Cancer Is All Mine

Cancer [noun]—a mysterious illness, believed to be contracted by making reference to its name.

The Complete Dictionary of Incomplete Truths

This isn't a book about me. Why would any of you want to read a book about me? This also isn't a book about cancer. Why would any of you want to read a book about cancer? What this is, is a book about me and cancer (why any of you would want to read a book about that, is a good question, one to which I hope that by the end of this book you'll have a satisfactory answer). *My* cancer. And that's something else altogether. My cancer is all *mine*, and no one can take that away from me. Considering the fact that multiple myeloma is chronic—incurable and recurring—that statement is true in the most literal sense, medically speaking. But that's not what I mean. What I mean is that it's *my* cancer, and therefore I reserve the right to express my thoughts about all matters regarding it, in the manner of my choice. And that's exactly what this book is. It's me saying what I want and how I want about my cancer. Without offending anyone, of course. Well, without intentionally offending too many people, I hope.

The first thing they tell you—after "I'm Doctor X and you are [drumroll...] a cancer patient!"—is that every cancer, every person, and every person's cancer is different. Different (and the same) bodies react differently to different (and the same) illnesses, and different (and the same) illnesses react differently to different (and the same) treatment. The key word being "different." And "the same." And while this pearl of personalized peril is primarily a reference to one's medical condition, I find it an equally suitable expression of the inevitability and legitimacy of each patient's individual mindset. And though all cancers are not created equal, one thing we cancer patients do share is our cancer-given rights, including freedom of cancer speech.

When it comes to cancer, people are very sensitive. Actually, that's not accurate. When it comes to cancer, people are very, *very* sensitive. Probably more so than regarding almost anything else. What other thing exists that ordinary, generally non-superstitious people are afraid to refer to by name? "The illness." "The big C." "He's not very well." What other phenomenon is so scary, and possesses such "that-which-shall-not-be-named" qualities, that its mere utterance evokes fear? As though, in some inexplicable way, the very mention of it has the power to inflict its horror on those who dare speaketh it. "Don't say it—you might catch it! Of course that's how it works! You don't believe me? I dare you to say it. Aaaggghhh, I can't believe you said it! Be gone, ye devil, and thy wicked word ways."

And perhaps, to a certain extent, it's justified. After all, in many cases, many cancers have put many people through many horrific experiences, often debilitating, torturing, and all too often untimely killing their hosts in a variety of excruciating ways, leaving behind devastated families and friends.

But "many" isn't most and "many" isn't all. And "many," most certainly, isn't me. There's only one person who has experienced my cancer, for better and worse, and that's me. And as me, I claim the exclusive right to suffer, complain, despair, cheer up, complain a bit more, but mainly to make fun, in my own way, of my own cancer and cancer-related experiences. And no one can take that away from me.

I'm aware that it's possible, in theory, that some people might be disturbed by the idea of a casual and jokey attitude toward the subject, though I doubt that many, if any of those, will be cancer patients. More likely, if at all, they will be people whose lives have been affected by people whose lives have been affected by cancer. I'm allowing myself to write because I truly believe that nothing I'm about to write is in any way lacking in sense and sensitivity. I am in no way belittling, underestimating the extent of, or making light of anyone's experience with cancer and the web of consequences that the illness may have spun around their lives.

One of the first things I learned about cancer, or, to be precise, about people in regard to cancer, is that many people are relatively unaware of the broad scope of conditions that are generally amassed under the cancer umbrella. The word "cancer" immediately conjures up the heart-wrenching image of an emaciated, bald child with sunken eyes, perhaps on a poster with an equally heartbreaking caption. Granted, we would be monsters to react in any other way. To *that* image. But there's no reason to associate that, or any particular image, with so general a word as "cancer."

The cancer canopy is a very broad one. It is indeed "a group of diseases involving abnormal cell growth with the potential to invade or spread to other parts of the body…Over one hundred types of cancers affect humans." Over a hundred types. That's quite a group. And as with any group, despite the unifying qualities, the individuals are very, very different from one another. Tigers and Tabbies are both cats, but I would only want one of them as a pet (the tiger, of course).

In fact, when I was first diagnosed, I met with the professor of hematology at the hospital in which I was to receive treatment and was told that some doctors don't even refer to multiple myeloma as a cancer. I politely informed her that Wikipedia defines it as "cancer of plasma cells" and "a type of blood cancer in the bone marrow," to which she responded that she knows the author of that particular article, and it so happens that his father died of multiple myeloma, so he may have been biased in describing the disorder as such. I wasn't quite sure how redefining the condition as a "non-cancerous, parent-killing illness" was supposed to be a comfort. Indeed, it wasn't. But that was fine, because I wasn't seeking comfort, just information. An outline of what was to come, be it comforting or otherwise, a map of sorts, of the journey that I was to embark on, albeit not by choice. And, like any journey into the wild and unknown, it was to be an adventure featuring dark caves, beautiful landscapes, fear, good company, dense, maze-like forests, splendid sunsets, biting cold nights, and, hopefully, a return ticket at the end.

So, before reading on, be warned, be cautious, and be wary. But most importantly—be excited, and make sure to enjoy yourself, because if I managed to live through it with a smile, or at least look back at it that way, you should certainly be able to have some fun reading about it.

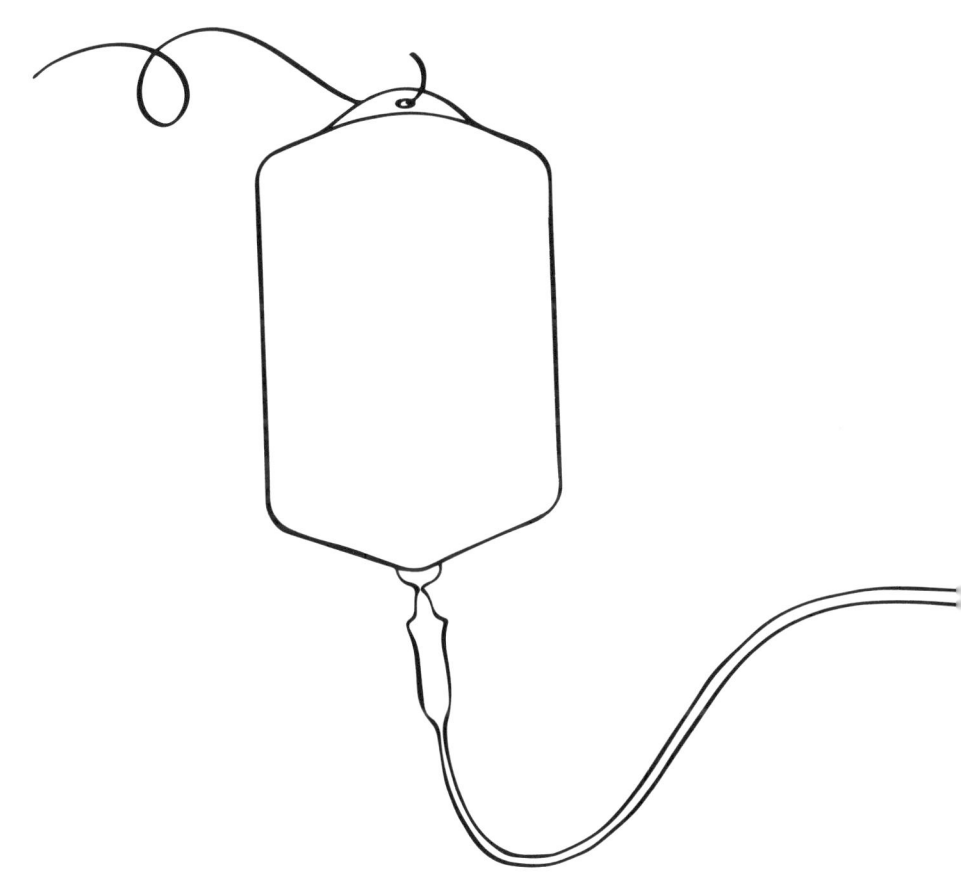

Part One

1
From So Simple a Beginning

It was the worst of times, it was the worst of times.

A Tale of Two Pities

All beginnings are hard. Except for the ones that are easy. And the ones that are so surreal that they're not really hard or easy, just surreal. This is my beginning.

One day, my wife commented that I was too skinny. I should see a doctor about it. I wondered how me seeing a doctor would cure her jealousy, but I chose to keep that witty tidbit to myself. With the passage of time and occasional repetition, this observation sank beneath the surface of conscious thought and joined the jumble of insignificant details that add up to the sum of one's general definition of self. OK, I'm a skinny person, so what?

Then, one day, my wife commented that I was too skinny *and* I hardly eat anything. I should see a doctor about it. See a doctor? *Real* men don't see doctors! They're way too busy doing more important men things, like maintaining archaic gender-based stereotypes about going to doctors. Time and repetition followed, and this observation too slid down the slippery slope of everydayness. It just became one of those things that come up in casual conversation from time to time: "Is sir ready to order?" "Oh, my husband doesn't eat much. A child-sized portion should be enough. Before you serve it, remove the side dishes and the drink, then split the main, and lastly, find someone else who's actually able to eat it, because all this talk of food has already filled his stomach to capacity."

Then, one day, my wife commented that I was too skinny *and* I hardly eat anything *and* I'm always tired. Tired? Well, obviously I'm tired—tired of hearing about how skinny and tired I am! I'll tell you why I'm tired: I have one wife, six kids, four jobs, and the only thing I exercise on a regular basis is my constitutional right to remain silent when asked if I exercise.

But this time she was on to something. I didn't think it was much of a something, but it was certainly something of a something. When you ask a bus driver why he spontaneously changed his route and circumvented your entire neighborhood, all fifteen stops, and he looks at you as though you've just barely mastered the art of forming a semi-coherent cognitive thought, you know you might be experiencing some difficulty staying awake. When you sit down to work at your computer, and the next thing you know, you're looking up at twenty pages of "zzzzz"s that you typed with your forehead, you know you're having a spot of trouble focusing on the job at hand. She was definitely on to something.

The thought that that something was cancer would have been, at that point, random at best. But that was tomorrow's news, and there was yet a long way to go until that day would arrive. At this point, why in the world would I think that my fatigue was caused by mutated white blood cells interfering with the production of red ones and resulting in anemia? How ridiculous would be the notion that my low appetite was the result of crumbling bones releasing calcium into my bloodstream. After all, I was just a bit thin and tired; surely one can't make much of a fuss about that.

So, I paid a courtesy visit to my doctor. I had to remind him who I was; we hadn't really kept in touch over the years. That tends to happen to healthy people, and to unhealthy people who think that they are healthy people. I didn't know what to expect, but suffice to say that he wasn't particularly impressed with my complaints. "Tired? Well, that's an easy one. I believe that you suffer from quite a common condition called 'life.' One is usually born with it, it tends to be chronic, and among its side effects is everything that will ever happen to you. Regarding the appetite, I can prescribe you some chocolate. It's perfectly legal in many countries and even available over the counter in some shops. It is, however, my duty to warn you about potential side effects. Happiness, for example is not uncommon."

Mission "small talk" accomplished, we moved on to business. He said I would have to take a blood test. "No need," I responded dismissively. "I've had it tested in the past and it was marked A+."

"A joker," he said, "I know the type. Let's take a look anyway, for extra credit."

The next morning, he called the house.

I had never received a call from a doctor before, and I had half a mind to say that I couldn't take the call now, but I have an available appointment some time in November. I decided against it, fearing the ever-so-slight chance that he might make the grave error, made by so many before him, of taking me seriously. I had a sneaking suspicion that he wasn't just calling to say he loved me.

"The results of your blood tests have arrived. Something interesting is up with your kidneys."

"Something *interesting*? Interesting as in 'It turns out that you have three kidneys ('primary,' 'backup,' and 'for sale'), how interesting!' or interesting as in 'Something interesting is up with your kidneys'? Aha. I see."

From there the ball picked up speed and started rolling. Downhill, some would say; into the pinball machine of life, I would put it. From my local doctor I moved on to a nephrologist, with a bit of biopsy-related help from a pathologist, after which I proceeded to a hematologist, and finally—an oncologist. It was safe to say that I was beginning to get the gist.

But it didn't happen quite that fast. My descent into decrepitude featured a few noteworthy highlights along the way:

- *Foam alone.* One of the key components of my diagnosis came about via a closer inspection of my urine (pardon the somewhat distasteful reference, but one of the many things one learns through extended medical experience is that nothing is sacred, not even your privacy, and certainly not your urine). The nephrologist sent me to do some initial tests and, upon my return visit, informed me that the protein content in my kidneys was a thousand times greater than it should be. Not the best thing in the world, but at that point still not cause for worry (not for him at least), he assured me. He wondered, though, if I had not perhaps noticed that my urine was extremely foamy. I had no clue what he was talking about, and, reaching into the deep void of my memory, I replied confidently that it was not. It was. And with my newfound awareness it didn't take long to verify. When I told my wife about this new and exciting discovery, she said that she had indeed noticed that the water in the toilet bowl was often foamy but had assumed that I was being unprecedentedly helpful and cleaning it daily with some sort of bubbly product. Till this day she laments the loss of the permanent freshly cleaned look her toilets once held, but such is the cost of living.

- *Blood is thinner.* Following the discovery of my kidney-function abnormality, a kidney biopsy was on the table. This routine and unalarming procedure was scheduled as a one-day event: the collection of a small sample by way of a quick jab to the lower back, and a few hours of rest to follow. In reality, the hospital extended its hospitality to ten days. Fortunately, while in the hospital, it was revealed that I suffer from a type of blood-clotting disorder, an insight that would undoubtedly be of great future value. Unfortunately, this discovery was made *after* the biopsy, not before, leaving me with a bleeding kidney. Hemophilia type C may not be as severe as its more "popular" co-disorders—type A and B (though it certainly makes up for it in "inclusiveness" by affecting both males and females equally)—but the medical team was nonetheless quite surprised to learn that I had never been made aware of my condition. "Have you never, by any chance, at any point in your life, bled to death?" they inquired politely. "No, I'm actually quite sure that's never happened. I think I would remember if it had. Well, to be accurate, I think other people would."
- *It's a kidney!* A couple of hours and three pints of internal bleeding later, I was sent for an ultrasound, to measure and monitor the

extent of the hemorrhage. This was truly a strange experience. Not unfamiliar, just strange. In fact, it was familiarity itself that made the experience so strange. Throughout the various stages of my wife's various pregnancies, I had been present during many ultrasounds, nodding "knowingly" at blurry and meaningless shapes on a monitor, as a technician pointed out what he claimed to be fetal feet and other imaginary images. "Sure. Whatever you say. Abstract art has never really been my strong side. Bottom line—there's a baby there, right? Great. See you again in two months." But now the tables—and all other furniture in the room—were turned, as I found myself lying on the bed, smeared in cold gel, while my wife stood peering into the screen. The atmosphere in the room was tense. After all, it's not every day you find yourself lying in hospital pajamas in a darkened room while a stranger prods your lower back with a plastic probe, waiting to find out if your kidneys are swimming in the shallow or deep end of the very local pool that has just been inaugurated within you. Now, there's a time and place for everything, and I knew this was neither the time nor the place. But the temptation was too great. There are some things that just have to be said, some words that just have to be set free; otherwise the world will not be complete. So, I looked the sonographer in the eye and asked, in the sincerest tone I could muster: "So, is it a boy or a girl?" I quickly learned two things about life: kidneys are genderless, and ultrasound technicians are humorless.

- *Scandalous.* That evening, a hospital attendant appeared in my room armed with a wheelchair. "I'm here to take you for a CT scan. Please hop in." Why a CT scan? Why a wheelchair? Why do I have no clue what's going on? These were but a few of the many profound questions that went through my mind in that moment. But not every question in life has an answer, certainly not one readily available. So, I took my seat and we set out on a journey through the labyrinth of hospital corridors, destination Computed Tomography (to follow up on the bleeding apparently). I imagine many of us are somewhat familiar with the general appearance of a CT scanner, be it from real life or from one medical drama or another. This was my first face-to-face encounter with this technological titan, and my reaction was simply: "So, they've finally pulled it off. They've invented a time machine." Goodbye, glasses, belt, and shoes; hello, past. I lay down, closed my eyes, and with great anticipation waited for the action to begin. The motorized "table" slid agonizingly slowly into the giant cylinder's mouth. I found myself in the belly of the beast, where much whizzing and whirling commenced. A disembodied robotic female voice emerged, instructing me, "Breathe," and "Don't breathe" (um, how long exactly am I expected to go without oxygen?), "breathe" (great, thanks). The whole experience culminated, however, in great disappointment; upon exiting the machine, I discovered that the time travel took place in a forward direction, and the time traveled was more or less the same amount of time that it takes to conduct a CT scan. Consequently, I did not in fact get to meet younger versions of myself and ponder such philosophical questions as "What was I thinking wearing that shirt?" and other mind-bending conundrums.

From there, the various clues paved the diagnostic path quite smoothly; the kidney biopsy showed permanent damage to the kidneys, the blood tests revealed anemia, and the CT scan unveiled bone lesions. The verdict was clear and was soon confirmed by way of bone marrow biopsy. I had multiple myeloma.

Not that I had the faintest clue what in the world that meant. But there would be plenty of time to learn about that later. For now, all I knew was that my journey had begun, and that at this point I had no idea where it was taking me. One thing I did know was that sometimes there is truth in what "they" say. They say that hospitals are no place for a sick person; you can catch all sorts of things there. How true. I went in perfectly healthy and came out with a blood-clotting disorder and cancer.

2
Check-Room-Mate

There once was a man in a room
Whose roommate was all gloom and doom.
As bad as it was
He complained not, because
His roommate's roommate was a buffoon.

Limericks for Sharing

In hospital rooms, as with any social order, there is a hierarchy, and, perhaps not unlike in the outside world, much of it is down to pure chance and timing. At the top of the room chain are people who somehow land themselves in private rooms. Below them are people who share a room and have the bed by the window. Below them are people who share a room and have the bed by the door. Below them are people who share a room and are neither by the window nor the door; rather, they've been slid between the two outer beds in a narrow curtained-off strip. Below them are the truly unfortunate—people whose beds are lined up along the corridors, eagerly waiting for some fortune-blessed room-dweller to heal or keel. I'm not sure if there's a level beneath that; it would have to involve being sprawled out on the parking lot floor and catching pills thrown from the ward window.

In this regard, when I was admitted for the kidney biopsy that would later, unexpectedly, lead to the discovery of my cancer, I was fortunate. I arrived at the hospital in the late evening of an early Motzaei Shabbos for what was meant to be a relatively short stay—some basic preparations, a morning biopsy, and an afternoon discharge. I found my way to the nurses' station of the ward I was scheduled to be admitted to and festively announced my arrival. The nurse on duty responded, somewhat less enthusiastically I must say, that they had no record of me in the system. "Are you sure you're booked in to have your procedure done here?" I think so. Or was it the Hilton or the local butcher I'd made a reservation with? Yeah, sure, I have a habit of just turning up at random hospitals with an overnight bag and a homemade map drawn on my lower back with X-marks-the-spot somewhere in the kidney area, wherever that is. You know what, since we're all here anyway, be a good sport and grab some sanitizer and that pair of scissors from the desk, and let's just get it over with. I could be home before bedtime.

"I'm sorry, sir, I wasn't told to expect you, and besides, there are no available beds currently. Not even in the corridor. Could I interest you in a lovely spot just outside the building, in the parking lot perhaps? You'll have to go home and return in the morning."

I was very unhappy with the prospect of traveling home and starting all over again the following day. I was already in the hospital-going mindset and had already said goodbye to the kids (in the temporary sense. The goodbye, that is, not the kids—they seem to be permanent). Though very unassertive and non-confrontational by nature, I felt that this was a situation in which standing up for myself was desperately called for. I stiffened my posture, looked the nurse straight in the eye with a confident gaze, and said, "Please?"

And so it came to pass that, instead of being admitted to corridor confinement in a somewhat gritty, hodgepodge, pre-everything ward, I was put up for the night, and—as it turned out—for the week, in a newly built, luxurious plastic-surgery unit, where I had not only a spacious and sparkly room, but pretty much the whole ward to myself. I put my belongings in the room and set out to explore the area. On my way out, I passed by the nurses' station and asked, naively and with complete sincerity, for the key to my room. The nurse, who most definitely had never before or since received such a ridiculous request, gave me a quizzical look, the equivalent of a whispered "Is this guy for real?" and reminded me that this was a hospital, not a bungalow colony. Fair play.

While in the plastic surgery ward, I was tempted to ask, seeing that I was there anyway and doing very little, if they could give me a quick makeover, just to spruce things up a bit before my facial skin went from "tailor made" to "loose fit." But I thought that was probably not how things work. And besides, I wasn't in the system.

A week later, quite bored, extensively tested, and plenty of internal bleeding the wiser, only a bone marrow biopsy short of being an official cancer patient, I was transferred—medically, mentally, physically, and very reluctantly—to hematology, where I was to meet my fate, and my roommate.

Hospital room-sharing brings up what I like to call "The Hospital Roommate Dilemma." The dilemma, simply put, is something like this: Considering the fact that soundproof nylon curtains have yet to be invented—and that no matter how hard you try you will have no choice but to listen to every word of their every conversation with a multitude of family members and visitors that defies spatial limits and always outnumbers yours—which is a better candidate for roommate: someone who converses using the traditional technique of speech, or someone who inexplicably does so using a curious method that involves a series of random sounds and incomprehensible grunts, known formally in linguistics as "other languages"?

With a same-language roommate, a significant portion of your attention will be constantly and involuntarily dedicated to taking in, or unsuccessfully attempting to block out, the tireless flow of brain-numbing chitchat that will undoubtedly be pulsating from the other side of the room, building up increased pressure on your skull and gradually seeping through the cracks of your sanity. You'll be privy to an array of precious nuggets of knowledge and wisps of wisdom, such as their level of satisfaction with Doctor X, Uncle Larry's latest argument-worthy comment, weather that's irrelevantly affecting the world outside the hospital room, and their eavesdropping roommate. Needless to say, this overload of unwanted and agitating mental activity is not particularly conducive to one's prescribed bedrest.

Such high levels of irritation will naturally lead one to wish for the alternative. At least with a foreign language, the sounds will surely merge into a smooth, fuzzy background noise that won't be received and processed and take up precious storage space in one's memory. This notion is akin to someone who is so fed up with being slapped in the face that they are excited at the prospect of being punched in the stomach instead.

To be honest, I personally love listening to foreign languages. There's a sort of a curious fascination to it—"How tuneful, how exotic, if only I could speak like that." That usually lasts for about two minutes. It soon turns into "How annoying, how different, if only I could stab myself in the ears with a screwdriver." You might, over time, become accustomed to the noise of a train driving through your neighborhood, rattling your house, perhaps even to the point of no longer noticing it at all. But it's a whole different story when the train is driving through your head, rattling your brain.

The worst part is that this already aggravating situation is accompanied by a profound and sobering realization: this is what *I* must sound like to almost all of the other eight billion people in the world. I am, universally speaking, an irritating person, purely by virtue of my verbal existence. Indeed, deep running and intertwined are the scars left upon mankind by the collapse of the Tower of Babel.

My roommate turned out to be of the other-language-speaking variety. Though, to be honest, throughout all our time "together" I never heard him speak a word. Only two types of noise emerged from behind the separating curtain. The first was courtesy of his brother, who never left his side, and had the TV on twenty-four hours a day, seven days a week, broadcasting a variety of programs in (un)said other language, one that apparently doesn't have words for basic concepts such as "earphones," "mute," "consideration," and "shut up, already!" The other noise that broke its way through the sound barrier of social acceptability was the nocturnal rumble known as snoring.

It's a funny thing, snoring. It's rare that you hate someone for doing something that they don't even know that they're involuntarily doing.

But you still do. Snoring is just one of those things that register high on the irritability scale and, in the case of my roommate, on the Richter scale.

In my high school dormitory we had a simple and mostly effective solution to this problem, one that didn't even require getting out of bed. Any offender was subject, by law of the lads, to the "shoe-throwing treatment." The procedure was quite straightforward:

1. If at any point during the night snoring is detected, reach down and fumble in the dark for your shoe. Proceed to throw the shoe in the general direction of the source of the noise.
2. If the noise persists, repeat the process with your other shoe, and so on and so forth with any other form of footwear in reach.
3. Once out of pedal props, use a series of sleepy grunts to indicate that the responsibility has been passed on to the next bed-dweller.
4. Follow this pattern around the room in a clockwise motion, until the snoring has ceased.

The system wasn't without flaw, though. Some mornings we would rise after a sleepless night, the room still reverberating with obnoxious rumbles, only to find the unfazed felon still blissfully asleep and sleepfully blasting, buried under a pile of shoes.

I wasn't quite sure if this was standard procedure in hospitals too, so to be on the safe side I kept my flip-flops to myself and asked the brother to turn up the volume on the TV in order to drown out the noise.

I never did find out what my roommate was in for, or what happened to him in the end. A few days into our non-relationship, upon returning from one test or another, I found that he was gone, never to be seen again. The brother's doing well, though. He's still there, as far as I know, still watching TV at a deafening volume. His shoes seem to be missing, however. I think they're probably somewhere behind my bed.

3
The Cards We're Dealt

Aces and kings reign supreme, but no deck is complete without jokers.

The Art of the Awkward Shuffle, p. 54

In a generation of digital communication, receiving "regular" post is a rare event. Even rarer is to receive something of any interest. Most of our post (i.e., bills) has long ago been converted to email, and most of us would happily forgo the multitude of junk mail ("rubbish post" just doesn't quite sound right) promising eternal happiness if we just buy/donate/support/enroll in this, that, or the other. As such, many of us don't bother visiting our local post box all that often, though for mysterious reasons that appear to be deeply rooted in our human need for excitement, constant stimulation, and a yearning for a sense of purpose and meaning in life, we still find ourselves profoundly disappointed each time we flip open the box only to find it empty.

But on one particular partly sunny and partly cloudy day, a surprise awaited me. There was no warning, no prior notice. Just like that, resting innocently between someone else's electricity bill and a twenty-page letter in three copies from the bank about paperless post and saving the environment. In the envelope, folded inside a single sheet of paper, was a small white plastic card. "We hereby inform you, that as of receiving this letter, you are medically and legally 100 percent disabled, and here's the card to prove it."

A hundred percent disabled? I took a quick peek at my legs. They didn't look any less functional than before. I took a tentative step forward, not sure what to expect. Everything seemed to be in order. I did a few jumping jacks (OK, one jumping jack), and then, breathing heavily, looked back down at the letter. Strange, but I guess I had no choice but to come to terms with the new reality.

After rapidly going through the five stages of grief according to the classic model—denial (no), anger (no!), bargaining (no?), depression (no…), and acceptance (yes), I settled down and read the rest of the letter, to find out more about my rights and benefits as a card-carrying cancer patient with 100 percent medical disability. One thing was quite clear—they weren't much. To be precise, two things, and two things only, were about to change in my life, and two very specific things at that:

1. As the proud owner of the card, I was entitled to cut to the front of any spontaneously generated queue, except for those that I wasn't entitled to. Nor was I entitled to any information regarding the criteria according to which this distinction would be made. I imagine that somewhere deep in the bowels of some government office complex there is a secret station where the coveted information is available, but I suspect that the queue there, which is made up exclusively of queuing exemptees, is quite long.

2. The second privilege awarded to me as a cardholder was free entrance to zoos and museums. Not for me, though. As it turns out, having cancer and being disabled do not warrant such a privilege. The aforementioned free entrance was offered to my caregiver or accompanier, whose services I would apparently require in order to maximize my visiting experiences, perhaps by offering such insightful comments as "I think the one behind the large boulder is a lion," or "Rembrandt, perhaps?" I made a mental note to find such a person, just in case I ever had the urge to visit a museum, pay full price, and grant someone else free admission.

What wasn't made clear in the letter was if one could combine both benefits, or was there a "no double discount" policy, as there often is at end-of-season sales. What if, for example, I wanted to cut the line at a zoo, *and* have my son (sorry, caregiver) enter free of charge? Would I have to choose the cheaper of the two benefits? Come to think of it, was my caregiver even entitled to the line-cutting privilege himself, or would I have to wait for him at the front of the line to award him his free admission? What would happen, for instance, if I were to team up with an equally abled disabled acquaintance and visit a museum: would we both be eligible for fee-free admission in our capacity as each other's accompaniers, or would our accompanying abilities deem us mutually unfit to bestow upon each other any disability-based privileges? As far as I know, these probing questions, and many others like them, remain unanswered till this day.

    Did I use it? Well, I thought some of you might be wondering that. Honestly, I never felt quite comfortable enough to take advantage of it. Sitting in a crowd of people, all impatient, bored, and with very low tolerance for queue-cutters—licensed or otherwise—I always decide against it. I've only used it once, and even then, mainly to satisfy the itch of curiosity—*I wonder if it really works?* I think it was time, place, and circumstance appropriate. We were at the city council, waiting in line to update my status and recognize my newly established disability. It was early on in the treatment days, when my body was still adjusting and showing significant signs of weakness. But still, marching proudly to the management desk and proclaiming, "Rush me in, for I am the disabled one!" just didn't feel right. So my wife told me to sit down and look weak. She approached the manager and flashed the card. The manager flashed me a look. I flashed a smile. It all happened in a flash, really. Then there was a pause. I'm not quite sure that she was quite sure what to do, or if and what the proper procedure was. After seconds of unbearable suspense, we were ushered into a back room where we were dealt with in a speedy and pleasant manner, with the customary blessings for good health and all, and that was pretty much it. An hour or so of waiting saved, an experiment conducted, and a moment of excitement over the knowledge that the card, never to be used again, actually works.

A few weeks later, another letter arrived, very much in the same unannounced manner as the first, this time informing me that my disability status had been revoked. Apparently, I was much better. I was very relieved to hear. A few weeks later another letter arrived, this time with a new card, informing me that my disability status had been reinstated, with all the perks and promise of line-cutting zoo-visits, only to be followed by another letter—yes, you guessed it—informing me that my status had been re-revoked. After this I was to receive one final letter, with one final card, to date. So, at present, for the third time in a short while, I am again the proud owner of a disability card, all two privileges included.

One would think that by this point I would be frustrated, somewhat fed up with the repeated excitement and disappointment of obtaining and losing my precious rights, the ups and downs of the emotional roller coaster I was being forced to ride. Perhaps, one may even suspect, someone high up in the operational wing of the state department of zoo-queueing was having a laugh at my expense. But I'll let you in on a little secret. The joke's on them. On the third card—the one that's currently "active"—the expiration date, usually a seven-year stretch, is, how shall we say, somewhat unusually extended. I am, by law, the proud owner of a disability card that will expire no earlier than the year 2699. So, I think it's safe to say, the last laugh is on them. Because in 670 years, when they and their great-great-great-great...grandchildren are long past their expiration date, I'll still be cutting lines in zoos and museums and granting spontaneous free entry to whoever happens to be standing behind me in line.[1]

Such are the cards we are dealt by life.

---

1 Note to any government officials who may be reading this: the above is not a formal and legally binding admission of holding an unauthorized disability certificate and illegitimate use thereof. And even if it were, which it isn't, it would be your fault. If such a card did exist, and I'm not saying that it does, I would appreciate if I would be allowed to keep it, since it's a valuable comedy prop, and in a world in which laughter is at times a rare commodity, every precious bit counts.

4
Food for Thought

An army that marches on its stomach will very likely cause damage to its internal organs, and generally speaking should probably go on a diet.

War and Piece of Cake, p. 789

Food, food, glorious food.

Shortly before receiving my diagnosis, we had relocated to a new city. Needless to say, the stress levels were quite high. One particular relative thought it appropriate to enlighten me with a piece of worldly wisdom asserting that the three most stressful things in life are illness, moving house, and losing a close one, and I was currently dealing with two of the three. I wasn't quite sure where he was going with this anxiety-axised trivia gem, or if he was planning on completing the full set for me.

Considering the importance of a community's support during difficult times, we were quite distressed at having just lost ours, and not particularly optimistic about the prospect of our future community coming to the aid of complete strangers. At this point, we knew almost no one, not even by name, and we certainly didn't yet have any form of meaningful relationship with them.

We were wrong. Our friends-to-be showered us with love and care, showing true kindness and, generally speaking, good neighborliness. First and foremost, this care came in the form of food. Food, which may have once been primarily a necessity-driven, energy-supplying commodity, has long since transcended this technical function and been elevated into the realm of culture, social interaction, pastime activity, antidepressant, and anxiety reliever. And who doesn't like food? Well, me for starters, but that was beside the point. Or perhaps that was exactly the point.

At the time, not knowing anyone by name, our food-based encounters with our new community were the only real introduction we had, and we resorted to referring to people (among ourselves, mainly) by their food-contribution names. And so, we had the honor of meeting Mr. and Mrs. Green-Beans, Mr. Potatoes, and Mrs. Spaghetti-and-Meatballs. In fact, at one point it seemed as though most of our new acquaintances were called Mr. and Mrs. Spaghetti-and-Meatballs, perhaps due to family ties or a secret cancer-healing recipe. This made it quite hard to tell them apart, and we had no choice but to resort to hyper-hyphenating them, using a sauce-based system. "Did you see what Mr. and Mrs. Spaghetti-and-Meatballs-with-Spicy-Tomato-Sauce brought this evening? What a sweet couple."

As this gesture of gastronomic generosity took to greater and greater portions and proportions, I soon developed what I call "The Cancer Guilt Complex." The Cancer Guilt Complex, simply put, is the notion that "I'm not worthy." Granted, people in difficult situations can hope for and "expect" help, and I'm certainly grateful and proud to be a member of Team Human, a special group that, as a whole, can boast a highly developed sense of morality. But I was troubled by the kindness that was extended toward us, on two accounts:

First, I truly felt undeserving of the extent of the support we received. After all, from my point of view, at least initially, nothing had really changed other than the fact that I was now labeled a cancer patient. The treatment I was receiving at that point was "relatively minimal," at least in comparison to what was to come. Its effect had not yet accumulated, and I was functioning more or less as before (which doesn't say much). I could, in theory, still cook myself a meal, to whatever extent I would (or probably wouldn't) have done before. So why in the world did I deserve such favor? Now I was not only a cancer patient, but a guilt patient too.

But my second issue was what really gave me no mental rest. My original feelings of unworthiness and guilt steadily graduated into a criticism of society's treatment of sympathetic causes. This contemplation was perhaps shameful and bordered on ingratitude, but it was fueled by sincere reflection. I was truly troubled by the disproportionate attention given to different charitable causes. In essence, it's a simple distinction: there's cancer, and then there's every other thing that could possibly happen to a person. Cancer, with its magically ominous power, transforms the way people relate to you, with absolutely no proportion to the actual extent of the effect the condition has on your life. It doesn't matter if nothing, or not much, in your daily routine has changed. The cursed crown of cancer has been placed upon your head, and that's all that matters. CANCER! It's the big C. And the big A. And the big N. And, you get the point. What else needs to be said? Nothing, apparently.

To "demonstrate" my point, I posed the following thought experiment: What would happen if, for example, my wife, God forbid, broke her leg? What reaction would that inspire? I'd like to think that on some level our social circle would come to our aid. Perhaps some minimal culinary courtesy would be extended. I doubt many or any sympathetic house calls would be made. But why? Surely, in terms of the effect these two occurrences have on our lives, my wife's hypothetical broken leg would be a much more crippling experience. Considering the fact that she does most of the household chores (and a few more), we would be in dire straits and in real need of help, whereas my actual cancer, at that point, had little effect on the physical smooth running of our family life.

But it wouldn't matter, because cancer is Cancer with a capital C, and the occurrence of a broken leg is just, how shall we put it, a lower case. The word is scary, the associations are scary, and that's just how people react.

Then my wife broke her leg.

Well, to be accurate, it was her foot. And to be really pedantic, it didn't break; I broke it. I know what you're thinking, and no, I didn't do it as a social experiment. It just happened, and I'll let you be the judge of it: One fine day, upon my wife's "initiative" (i.e., command), we were rearranging a bookcase on which photos were arranged along the top shelf. As I was moving some books, I knocked over a photo frame. For reasons that are beyond my comprehension, the manufacturers of this particular picture frame thought that it would be a good idea to make it from stone, with rough edges, sharp corners, and considerable heft. Now, clumsy I may be, but I'm not totally heartless; as this deadly weapon plummeted toward the general area of my wife's bare feet (she doesn't believe in shoes, as real as they may seem to the rest of us), I just about managed to shout out, "Don't move!" somehow intuitively confident that the picture would fall, by default, next to her foot, but surely not on it. Then came the scream. I turned to see my wife on the floor, a blood geyser spurting from her foot where the sharp corner had left its mark. Her exact words were (after the initial: "AAAHHH!!!"), "IT HURTS SO MUCH! IT'S LIKE GIVING BIRTH THROUGH MY FOOT. WITHOUT AN EPIDURAL!" I can certainly vouch for that. I've been there six times (in the delivery room, that is). It certainly sounded the same. And, much like in those similar experiences, the help I was able to offer was very minimal (i.e., nonexistent), and I would have much rather been waiting outside.

What came next involved three emergency service men, a stretcher, fifty-one stairs down, an ambulance, a hospital visit, and fifty-one stairs up, with a bandaged broken foot the only product of her labor. (There was more to it, but much like my wife's foot, you get the picture.)

Much like in the Garden of Eden, it was all her fault, of course. Who rearranges furniture without shoes? Who fails to notice a picture frame falling, doesn't immediately jump back, and doesn't process and ignore a "don't move" instruction? And mainly, who marries a clumsy Muppet like me?

But all this was beside the point. The good news, regarding which my wife somehow failed to share my excitement, was that now we could test my hypothesis and prove me right.

As it turns out, I was wrong. And I was right. I was more wrong than I expected, but righter than I would have liked to be. Our community renewed its charitable activities and generously provided cooking and babysitting support. But it was hard not to notice that it lacked the drama and scope of the earlier "cans for cancer" project. There's not much we can do about it; society reacts to situations emotionally, not rationally. And, to be honest, in the grand scheme of things, we're probably better off that way. I'm not sure I would like to live in a world that functions according to the rules I want the world to function according to. A society that measures everything in a cold and rational way and robotically produces purely functional and mathematically appropriate responses doesn't sound like a great place to live in. True, in some cases there isn't a perfect correlation between the receiver's needs and the giver's deeds, but ultimately the world is a better place for it, much more human.

In conclusion, I can say that I learned two valuable life lessons from the whole experience: people are great, and I'm a philosophically inclined ungrateful grump.

5
Knock, Knock

Knock, knock. Who's there? Your neighbor. Your neighbor who? Your neighbor who really dislikes you but presents a façade of friendliness in order to avoid the awkwardness of sharing a communal living space with you. Oh you, do come in.

Jokes to Knock Your Socks Off

Hi, sorry, but I don't have any to spare right now; I'm just in the middle of something; I'm not home; I'm not interested; I already gave at work."

Traditional greeting

One thing life has taught me is that "neighborhood" and "neighbor-hood" are two very different things.

We've always lived in good neighborhoods, but in recent years, in terms of immediate neighbors, we've always seemed to have landed on the wrong side of friendly. For many years we lived on a yeshiva campus in a close knit community, enjoying its uniquely warm social bonds and pleasant familial atmosphere. With time, however, our family outgrew our small apartment, our commercial needs outgrew the provisions of the one local shop, and our kids outgrew the point where they were content with a cowshed being the height of local entertainment. And so, we moved to the big city (a modest and mostly abandoned village would be considered a metropolis in comparison to our previous location).

Fortunately, our new neighborhood turned out to be friendly enough. With the small exception of our new downstairs ground-floor-dwelling neighbors, who apparently didn't share the universal moral imperative "Do unto others that which isn't absolutely horrible." This Olympian, golden-aged, silver-haired, bronze-faced, stone-hearted couple was used to their quiet home environment and had difficulty adjusting to sharing the world with our six-pack of young, spirited children. After perfecting their death stare, they advanced to verbal unfriendliness and frequently complained about the disruption of their daily siestas. How dare our children play in our apartment between the hours of "first thing in the morning" and "any time earlier or later." I was tempted to return the favor when they took up the curious practice of midnight gardening beneath our bedroom window, but I decided to not be rash and sleep on it first, which was, naturally, particularly challenging.

Our unneighborly relationship reached its peak low one otherwise fine day when the conveniently named Mrs. Downstairs called to "ask" if we could please come down immediately and clean up a suspicious bit of excrement that had appeared in their garden. Through some manner of masterful Sherlockian deduction, she had reached the conclusion that it was surely "placed" there by one of our children. The somewhat curious fact that her extraordinary accusation required believing that the hypothetical offending subject managed the remarkable acrobatic feat of projecting the very-not-hypothetical offensive substance through our balcony safety bars and far out into their garden did not drive her to consider an alternative, perhaps slightly less absolutely unrealistic explanation. I wondered if as a child her "First Words" book was missing the "D for dog" page, or perhaps in her edition D was for "Do not love thy neighbor." Granted, one of my toddlers did occasionally water a small portion of their garden, free of charge, from said location, but *she* didn't know that (and neither did I at the time, of course, added my lawyer). Though the extremely lush rose bush directly beneath our balcony might have been a giveaway.

We moved in the summer.

We relocated to a different building and, with a great sense of relief and hope, looked forward to our new neighboring prospects. We moved in, and things were going really well. Until the next morning. I arrived home from work to find my wife in tears. She relayed how, earlier in the day, there was a knock on our door. Excited for the much-anticipated warm welcome, she cheerfully rushed to open the door, only to be confronted, not with a cake, nor a smile, nor a "my name is so-and-so; welcome to the building," but with a "neighborly" complaint. Our new downstairs neighbor made her debut appearance with the following smashing hit: "Hello. In this building, we're very particular about cleanliness. Your rubbish bag has leaked all over the stairwell. My daughter almost stepped in it. Please clean it up immediately." She then proceeded to turn abruptly, walk away, and mutter "to herself," very much audibly, "Disgusting."

Needless to say, this was not quite the greeting my wife was hoping for. I was particularly outraged, since I knew with certainty that the spillage was not "ours." I had noticed it that morning when I left for work. Being the official and exclusive take-out-the-rubbish-er of the home, I was confident that it didn't originate from our house. It certainly wasn't the result of a deed performed by one of our children. It couldn't have been. Judging by their "where it is used, there it shall forever rest" policy, they don't even seem to know where we keep the bin. On the rare occasions when they do seem to stumble upon it (perhaps by pure chance when incidentally snacking over its air space), or sporadically decide to follow the rules of shared living space, they seem to be oblivious of a different set of rules, namely gravity. I believe it was Newton's fourth law of motion that stated that "a tower of rubbish rising high above and far beyond the capacity of its receptacle will, at some point, start moving with great speed toward the kitchen floor, causing much splash and mass mess." To consider the possibility of one of the kids taking on the titanic task of taking out the bin would require not only a whole new set of laws, but a suspension of the entire concept of the basic principles of natural order. There is no shortage of spillage in the Emmett village, but this particular one just wasn't one of ours.

But this was beside the point. Guilty or not guilty, there are ways to go about things. I firmly believe that people have the right to be wrong, but they have a responsibility to be wrong in the right way.

Though not at all assertive by nature, I felt that this sort of behavior should not go without an appropriate response, and perhaps some questionably inappropriate reprimand. I decided to confront her. With a note. Taped to her front door. While she was out. That's as far as my passive-aggressive disposition would let me take things. It read: "Dear Mrs. X (strangely, she hadn't introduced herself, and there was no name on the door), Thank you for bringing the 'suspicious spill' scandal to our attention. I too am an avid believer in cleanliness, particularly in regard to one's conscience. I'm quite sure that yours is clean, as it appears that you have never used it. I know firsthand that we were not responsible for the spillage, and regardless, it would have been appreciated if your rude and false accusation was prefaced by some preliminary welcoming words and a warm, albeit fake, smile. Wishing us all a socially sanitary week. Yours truly, Mr. Upstairs."

I really didn't want to make enemies so soon after moving in, but it didn't seem that she was planning on making friends, so there probably wasn't much loss involved, give or take a few uncomfortable path-crossings in the communal stairwell, which, incidentally, I had since cleaned.

At the end of the year, we moved again.

Our new apartment building neighbors didn't disappoint and maintained the reception procedure that seemed to be standard in every house we move into. Moreover, this time they really outdid themselves and reached new and unprecedented heights, breaking all past records of the international unfriendly neighbors competition. In truth, I'm not even sure the term "neighbors" is accurate here, since the complaints came rolling in while our furniture was still in the process of rolling out of the removal truck. The movers were carrying our belongings up the fifty-one stairs that led to our apartment, grumpily but at an unnaturally fast pace, creating a constant stream of boxes, electrical appliances, and other belongings. We scrambled in a futile attempt to channel each new arrival to its designated room, trapped in a giant real-life game of Tetris in which we desperately moved items to one side or another before the next one arrived and blocked the route, fearing that at any moment the living room floor might be filled and the house would disappear. While all this was taking place, we were visited by three of our neighbors-to-be. The first complained that one of our children was making noise in a close-by park. Thank you *so* much for bringing that to my attention; I'll just pop down this fridge and see to it right away. The second complained that one of the movers was smoking a cigarette outside the building, right under the No Smoking sign. (In his defense, the sign wasn't very visible. It was obscured by smoke.) The third complained that we had placed our empty cardboard boxes on the wrong side of the communal bins, a grave unboxing offense indeed. Suffice to say, we were off to a rocky start.

A few days later, however, the building earned some degree of redemption, as an elderly ground-floor gentleman clambered up the stairs to our apartment and presented us with a homemade smile and a cake to match. It turns out that there is indeed hope for mankind, and it's covered in a thick layer of chocolate icing.

I soon noticed something interesting about our new building. None of the apartment doors had name signs on them, as is customary in most local apartment complexes. I mused over how this small gesture, or lack thereof, was very telling, and revealing of the residents' attitude toward potential visitors and newcoming neighbors. It's quite hard to form any form of relationship with someone who isn't even willing to provide you with their identity. I later noticed that only one front door boasted a floor mat. It sported the word "welcome," but was (and still is, years later) placed in the wrong direction, technically welcoming people out, not in as its designers probably intended. More of an unwelcome mat than a welcome one. It was probably unintentional, but it fit the local attitude of unfriendliness very nicely. We were insistent on breaking the local custom of cold corridor conduct and put up a sign with our name, but out of respect for the residents' tradition we settled on the following, not entirely insincere shop-bought signs: "If I were you, I wouldn't go in," and "Forget about the dog; beware of the owner."

As time went by, a deeply troubling thought crept into my mind. We had lived in three different places, within the short span of three years, and in all three cases found ourselves surrounded by bad neighbors. Keeping in mind the law of probability, could it be possible, by any chance, that *we* were the bad neighbors? I soon dismissed this absurd notion. Of course not. This was in no way a biased perspective; it was a purely mathematical deduction. The exact same statistical law determined that every story is more likely to have only one, rather than two sides.

Now, some sharp-eyed readers may have noticed that we're almost at the end of a long chapter, and the star of the show, the cancer character, hasn't made an appearance. Some of you may be wondering if, when, and how it's going to enter the picture. Well, don't worry. From the moment cancer makes its first appearance, it's pretty much always in the picture, even if sometimes you have to squeeze it in. Benjamin Franklin (and a couple of others who beat him to it but weren't fortunate enough to be popularly credited for it or feature on one-hundred-dollar bills) famously wrote that only two things are certain—death and taxes. But I would wager that a close third is the almost certainty that introducing cancer into a conversation will have some effect on just how comfortable that conversation becomes. Be it an ice-maker or an ice-breaker, it's always a conversation shaker. On that fateful first day when we moved into our current residence, it led to our least negative interaction. One neighbor did stop by and introduce himself. My wife referred to me, as she often did in those early illness days, as "my husband, who has cancer." "Oh," he said. "My mother had cancer. She died."

And a good day to you, too, sir.

6
Cry as You May

Crying [noun]—the bodily function of producing and shedding tears, eliciting a variety of reactions from men: when performed for the first time by a baby—celebration; on subsequent occurrences—irritation; when performed by a woman in his presence—a very uncomfortable feeling and the general sense of not knowing what to do; when experienced by man himself—confusion.

The Complete Dictionary of Incomplete Truths

Fears and tears are, naturally, not uncommon in the context of a serious illness and any other similarly challenging circumstance that involves uncertainty. Personally, throughout the various stages of my illness, I can say, without a hint of shame, that I indeed experienced both. I can also say, without a hint of pride, that I experienced each of these only once, at least memorably. I can also say, without a hint of ambivalence, that I believe that there's a lesson to be learned from both occasions (which is not to say that I indeed learned these lessons. But if I can't practice what I preach, should I not at least practice preaching?).

The two instances took place at the very start of my cancer tales, and both involved the telling of cancer. After a week in the hospital, on a Friday afternoon, a doctor I hadn't previously encountered walked into my room and sat down. He introduced himself and said that the results of the bone marrow biopsy had arrived and there was a clear diagnosis.

You would think that the words that followed this introduction would be etched into my memory, and that I would be able to repeat and report them verbatim. But all I remember is that by some clever and considerate use of words he managed to drop the bomb so softly that it was disarmed before it even landed. We spoke for a few minutes, though once again my memory seems to have scrubbed that content. Before standing up to leave, he gestured toward my tablet and said, "Do yourself a favor, don't google it." He left the room, his words trailing behind him and echoing in my ears, "...google it, google it." To be honest, at that moment in time, searching for "multiple myeloma" wasn't easy for me. Not for emotional reasons, simply because after having heard the condition's name only once, I wasn't familiar enough with it to repeat it, and had to search several words that bore a vague assonance to what I recalled hearing before finding what I wanted. I use the phrase "finding what I wanted" quite loosely here, as I would hardly describe a Wikipedia article reporting a life expectancy of three to five years as something I "wanted to find."

I'd like to believe that by this point it is evident to the reader that there have been many experiences and moments in my journey that have been either funny, or potentially funny, or serious with a chance of being made funny. This experience was none of the above. It was an utterly unique stand-alone moment in a long series of unordinary moments. I'm quite confident that given five minutes of concentrated effort, from the safe perspective of the present, I could come up with a witty quote, a couple of jokes, and some arguably amusing wordplay related to thinking that you have three years to live, but to do so would be to dishonor the gravity of that moment and cheapen the tragedy of anyone who has experienced anything like it. The prospect of dying in my thirties and leaving behind a wife and six children aged ten and under wasn't a laughing matter then, when it was real, and isn't now, when it's not.

Thank God this horror didn't last long. I tracked down the doctor and asked him, in simple terms, "WHAT?!" He reassured me that this prognosis was absolutely wrong, or to be accurate, simply outdated. Within the span of one decade, the advances made in the treatment of multiple myeloma have been so significant that the condition has been redefined as "merely" chronic and not terminal. My life expectancy, he informed me, was exactly what it would otherwise be (though he did not elaborate, at that time, on the subject of exactly what that life would look like. There would be plenty of time for that later, apparently, and hopefully).

I imagine it's not particularly common to thank God for going through a difficult experience without any support, but I am sincerely grateful that I was completely and utterly alone at that moment and hadn't yet shared any news with anyone, so no one else had to go through those same moments of terror. By the time I did share the news, I was armed with the disclaimer and a positive prognosis, once again learning that although bad is never great, it's always better than worse.

While that fateful Shabbos was ushered in with fears, I bid it farewell with tears. My wife, who had been with me in the hospital during the days of that week, had already gone home to spend Shabbos with the kids before the doctor dropped in with the diagnosis, leaving me with the task of sharing the news with her. I had no clue what the right way to do this was, but I had a strong feeling that telling her over the phone, leaving her to spend Shabbos alone with the kids and the news, was the wrong way. I made it through our phone call before Shabbos without disclosing anything incriminating.

Generally speaking, much like a proud business owner, I love my own company. Nevertheless, under the circumstances, I didn't think that spending Shabbos alone would be a great idea, so I invited my brother over for a sleepover. He readily obliged, and despite my best attempts at good hospitality, he insisted that I take the bed and he sleep on the pullout armchair. Mad as it sounds, it wasn't an entirely unpleasant experience. After all, Shabbos is Shabbos, family is family, and even when eaten out of small disposable containers on a hospital bed, cholent is cholent. Similarly, a shul is a shul, though a hospital shul is certainly a strange davening environment fashion-wise, in which anything goes. Praying side by side were people dressed in Shabbos clothes, weekday clothes, work clothes, various colors of scrubs and medical uniforms, hospital pajamas and gowns, and various combinations thereof. I don't recall which category I fell into at the time, but what I do remember, and always will, is my Motzaei Shabbos *Maariv* and the uncontrollable sobbing that accompanied it, easily putting the collective experience of a lifetime's worth of my Rosh Hashanah and Yom Kippur *tefillos* to shame.

This timing was not a result of me being careful not to cry on Shabbos, piously waiting till after *atah chonantanu* to resume weekday woe. It was because up until that point I was "fine," and only then, while praying for guidance regarding the wisest way to carry out the task of calling my wife, did the reality of having to share the news with her resurface. I imagine that over the years, many had stood at that exact spot, crying for their life, or praying for a loved one. But ultimately, I was doing neither, not in the classic sense. I was crying for the impact the new reality would have on my wife and praying for the strength to be her support, because if there's one thing that's immeasurably scarier than an illness, it's the illness of someone you love. Fortunately, when life gave me lemons, it also gave me an aid, but it consequentially appointed me as an aid, too, and with this great responsibility I needed to find within myself equally great power.

The first step in this process was, naturally, figuring out the best (aka least bad) way to relay the news. The truth is, it turned out that my wife was, characteristically, way ahead of me, at least in suspicion and worry and everything else. The truth is, when they told me that we were doing a bone marrow biopsy, I should have been wise to the implication. The discrepancy between our predictions was due to our different approaches to potential disaster. In general, people can be divided into three groups in this regard: those who assume the best outcome until proven otherwise, those who assume the worst outcome until proven otherwise, and those who assume the worst outcome even after proven otherwise. And then there's me—group of one: don't even think about it until it's a fact. Once it's a fact, do nothing about it for a while; then figure it out. So, in this respect, we were on opposite ends of the crisis continuum, something that often actually serves us well.

Still, the transition from fearing to knowing would naturally be a difficult one, and it was my job to figure out how to make it as smooth as possible.

If you're looking for sage counsel and solid advice on how best to deliver such news, God forbid, it's time for you to put this book down for a few moments, take some time for introspection, and ask yourself how it's possible that you haven't yet realized that I don't have the answers, and more often than not it's unclear if I even have the right questions. Now you can continue.

After making *Havdalah*, I contacted a highly regarded professional who had the relevant qualifications and experience, and asked for some tips on how to go about things. I still believed that doing it over the phone was a bad idea, mainly because it was a bad idea. I arranged that a good friend of my wife would randomly contact her and offer to accompany her to the hospital first thing Sunday morning, and we took it from there. I'm fully aware that "and we took it from there" might be the part that matters most here and that I've disclosed absolutely nothing about it, but as I said, look not to me for answers, but for a collection of confused thoughts and mild entertainment.

When it comes to fears, as a rule, don't let your fears rule you. And do yourself a favor—before spending too much time worrying to death about how to deal with a terrible situation in life, or any old problem, first make sure that you're right about something being wrong. And when it comes to tears, cry as you may, but try to be the reason for someone else to cry a little bit less.

7
The Future of Mankind

Kids—can't live with them, can't live on without them.

Other parents

As a son, I would gladly give a kidney. As a parent, I wouldn't hesitate to give two.

Kid Knees and Kid's Needs, p. 2

When it comes to the "if," "with whom," and "how" of sharing news of cancer, there are different schools of thought. I use the terms "schools" and "thought" loosely and quite generously here, since my sense is that some of the approaches are no more than educated guesses, or just mere instincts. Which is not to say that they are wrong. The assumption that school and thought are the correct answer to every question is itself not much more than an educated guess, or just mere instinct. Which is not to say that it's wrong. And so on.

Granted, every patient has the right to hide or share to the degree that is comfortable for them, according to their personal perception of their own condition and their natural tendencies, or just on a whim. But as a moral imperative, the feelings of others must be accommodated, too, on some level. And it's here, in the search for that delicate balance, that matters can get a bit sticky.

From day one, my wife favored a bomb-drop approach, one in which the sentence "This is my husband; he has cancer" became a standard introduction when meeting people for the first time, one that produced casual comments such as, "I'll be with you in a moment; I'm just saying goodbye to my husband. He has cancer. No, not that sort of goodbye—he's just popping out to the shops." Or "I'd like to make a dental appointment for my husband; he has cancer. Yes, the appointment that's surprisingly available this afternoon without the usual three-month wait will be fine, thank you." This unhesitant straightforwardness was her way of coping with our new reality, and I fully respected and accepted it. I can't necessarily say the same for those on the receiving end of these blunt blasts. Unsurprisingly, eyes opened wide and eyebrows raised high often featured on her victims' faces.

I myself, sensitive soul that I am, was more comfortable with a slightly more subtle approach. You have to break it to them slowly; it's only fair. "Good morning! How was your weekend?"

"It was actually really nice, thank you." Pause. "By the way, I have cancer." Longer pause.

This was all well and good when the recipients of our newsflash were grown-ups, people whose emotional stability we weren't worried about, or at least weren't responsible for worrying about. The big question was how to break the news to the kids. Some, perhaps more noble, cancer patients may choose to keep such information from their children, lest it traumatize them. But I was always taught about the importance of sharing, and besides, why suffer alone when other people can suffer along with you? More to the point, for one, there was the obvious challenge of keeping up such a lie by finding alternative explanations for spending two days a week in the hospital, daily steroid-induced mood fluctuations of horrible highs and loathsome lows, hair loss, temper loss, generally being at a loss, and a motley crew of other fun-packed side effects. But mainly, and much more significantly, there was the question of what was right, and we had no doubt that something that was about to become a central part of our lives should be shared with those who were a central part of our lives. The question was just how to go about it.

So, we sought professional advice, as one does. We met with a psychiatrist, a psychologist, and a social worker. Unfortunately, these meetings were separate and did not take place in a bar, so I can't boast a new joke. Much like peanuts at a bar, the advice offered by these experts was complimentary; unlike peanuts at a bar, the advice offered by these experts was not complementary. We received clear and confident instructions, in the form of a variety of conflicting recommendations: "Sit them down together" / "Address each one individually in accordance with his or her age"; "Explain the full extent of the illness in full detail" / "Just say that Daddy is a bit poorly"; "Keep them updated with each new development" / "Let things fade into subconsciousness."

Kids are always complaining, "Why do I need to learn math? What's it good for in the real world?" The honest answer to this question, cynics would say, is, "You're absolutely right, twelve years of school are not intended for the accumulation of practical knowledge; they serve as an extended intelligence test that filters a certain percentage of the population out of higher education, and to keep them occupied until they're old enough to go to university/college/the army/work/a Buddhist retreat/Mars. The real question isn't which subjects can we cut out, but how can we make the school day longer." Needless to say, I myself would never express such negative sentiments in writing. Either way, our counseling conundrum provided me with a rare and precious opportunity to demonstrate the real-life practical application of mathematics. Long years of study certainly helped me solve the following problem: If X is different than Y, and Y is different than Z, and X is different than Z, what can be deduced? Solution—that we have a problem. Correct answer, see page 441 for details. Or in other words, using fewer letters (many more letters, technically): now, after seeking advice, instead of knowing nothing, we knew too much, two points on the knowledge spectrum the distance between which can only be calculated by using infinity and other magic numbers (once again a victory for mathematics). Instead of being lost in the wilderness of ignorance, we were buried under a mountain of information. It was all very confusing, but we had to make a decision.

So, we did. We decided to ignore everyone's advice. As one does.

We went for the most simple and direct approach: "Kids, we need to talk to you. There's this thing, it's called cancer, and Aba has it. No, you can't have some; it's not that kind of thing. It's an illness. No, it's not contagious, but it will still affect the rest of us."

My oldest son, who was eleven at the time, immediately asked, "Aba, are you going to die?" I paused thoughtfully, contemplating whether this was a good time to teach him the facts of life (or death, more accurately), and replied, "Yes, but not anytime soon, and not from the cancer. Just a plain old-age death, one day in the far future. I'm sorry I can't provide a more positive, nature-defying answer, something that violates the second law of thermodynamics or whatever law it is that's responsible for entropy, everything turning into chaos, and us dying. But, as carbon-based bio-matter, we do tend to disintegrate, eventually." Immortality, like so many things in life, is only temporary.

After clarifying that small technical detail, we told our kids that they should feel totally comfortable asking anything they want to know about our family's news. "It's best to be open and not to repress any fears and develop anxieties," we told them. "Is there anything you want to ask Ima and Aba?"

"Um, there is, actually one thing," said their representative. "What we want to know is, well, could you by any chance move a bit to the side? You're blocking the computer screen." Case closed. Apparently, they had heard the one about the psychiatrist, the psychologist, and the social worker who walked into a bar, and didn't think it was award-winning material.

In general, we really don't give our kids enough credit. They may be small, but that doesn't mean they're stupid. The fact that their response to most statements and requests is "What do you want from me?" even when the instructions seem quite clear, doesn't exactly support this claim, but let's put that aside for the moment. Kids may be childish, but that doesn't mean they are not caring. The fact that "What do I care?" is their universal mantra doesn't do much for this claim either, but let's put that aside for the moment, together with the first query, in the enormous pile of mysteries labeled "Kids, what's their deal anyway?"

In fact, soon after receiving the news of my diagnosis, my young children proved to be both clever and compassionate.

One son, as we discovered several months later, showed great ingenuity, as he convinced his teachers that my cancer was a justifiable cause for a general exemption from all homework assignments. This was due, apparently, to the heavy load of housework that was now imposed on him. To this day we're still not quite sure exactly in which house this work was taking place, and how he managed to do it while keeping up his regular full schedule of doing nothing at all, at all times. But I have to hand it to him, he definitely deserves extra credit for creativity, though for some reason it didn't show on his report card.

Another son showed just how caring a young child can be. Upon learning of my illness, he became extremely concerned and worried. "But what if…oh, the thought is simply unbearable. What if…a dog had cancer? Somewhere in the world, some poor dog might be battling this terrible illness at this very moment!"

His google searches of "dog" and "cancer" revealed that not only can cancer find dogs, but dogs can also find cancer. Apparently, with their strong sense of smell, some dogs can sniff out cancer. "So that's that," he said. "It's settled. Now we surely need to get a dog." He seemed convinced that finally, years of fruitlessly begging for a dog had come to an end. I stood bewildered. Why in the world would we need a dog to tell us that I had cancer when we clearly knew that already? "But Aba," he protested. "The internet says that a dog can sniff the cancer right out of you. We *must* get one!" "Aha, I see. Sniff out cancer. I'm not sure that their sense of smell is *that* strong."

But in all seriousness, as much as we joke about kids—and in our house we do quite a bit of that—they are, aside from being the future of mankind, amazing little creatures. I'm not saying that they're easy; my six are definitely more than a handful. They are, at times, extremely challenging, perhaps justifying God's omission of "*ki tov*" on that fateful first Friday. But the bottom line is that they are the greatest work of art we can ever aspire to create, and it is our duty to help them be the best version of themselves (not *ourselves*) that they can be. I like to think of them as being a lot like, well, a lot like a lot of things. This is how I put it:

Kids are like kites, high in the sky
We unreel the string and hold on as they fly
At times the string gets tangled, or stuck in a tree
Kids are like kites, connected but free

Kids are like trees, we plant and they grow
We wait for the fruit, nature is slow
They thrive in the sunshine and rain we supply
Kids are like trees, they reach for the sky

Kids are like balloons, we must fill them with air
If we give them enough, they can go anywhere
But if we give them too much, they will certainly burst
Kids are like balloons, remember to stretch them first

Kids are like books that we have to write—
The pages and chapters—and make it sound right
But we don't get to decide how each story ends
Kids are like books, they come in many trends

Kids are like the moon, they reflect our own light
By day we outshine them, they glow in the night
But sometimes they seem to withdraw and to shrink
Kids are like the moon, bigger than we think

Kids are like birds, they must learn how to fly
At first they will fall, but we must let them try
And one day our birds will leave home, like the rest
Kids are like birds, and we are their nest

Kids are like houses we build from the start
And give strong foundations so they don't fall apart

But we don't get to choose the interior design
Kids are like houses, they host the Divine

Kids are like stars, they twinkle and shine
They give us a sense of direction and time
But sometimes they fall in the dark of the night
Kids are like stars, distant and bright

Kids are like water, fresh, pure, and cool
Stormy like a sea, still like a pool
Sometimes we feel that we're drowning below
Kids are like water, they teach us to flow

Kids are like dreams, they reflect how we feel
Fast and exciting, and a little unreal
At times unclear, and hard to understand
Kids are like dreams, not easily planned

Kids are like life, they have ups, they have downs
They bring about smiles, and also cause frowns
But we only live once, so we must do our best
Kids are like life; give love, have faith, Hashem will do the rest

Don't get me wrong. They're pretty irritating, too. But that's a subject for a different poem. For now, let's just enjoy them.

APPENDIX—COMICAL CULINARY COUNSEL

As far as I know, the joke about a psychiatrist, a psychologist, and a social worker who walk into a restaurant doesn't exist. So here goes:

> *A psychiatrist, a psychologist, and a social worker walk into a restaurant and sit at a table. The waiter comes over and asks, "Do you want to order?" "The real question," says the psychologist, "is not what we want, but what you yourself want." "OK," says*

the waiter, "so how can I help you?" "In order to help us," says the social worker, "we first have to accept that we need help and want to help ourselves." "I see," says the waiter. "So just some water for the table for the time being, then."

After the meal, the waiter comes over to the table and asks, "Can I interest you in a dessert? Some gourmet chocolates, perhaps?" "Just two tablets please; full stomach," responds the psychiatrist.

When the waiter brings the bill, he finds the table deserted, and a note written on a napkin: "Sorry, but we had to rush to a session with our next waiter. Here's the bill; please sort it out with our office. Mental health service not included."

8
Rhyme and Reason

"I have labored, and I have found." What I have found is that my labors are usually a colossal waste of time.

Tractate Emmett 6b

I always read two books, one non-fiction and one fiction—the former to better understand reality, the latter to escape it.

The Art of Double Booking, p. 2

"**Happiness** has no [wh]y." Indeed. But in keeping with the theme of this spelling pun-based profundity, "misery" does. Or at least we want it to. Suffering needs justification. Pain needs explanation. The "why" question echoes through the history of mankind, and many of the greatest thinkers have dedicated substantial portions of their time and brainpower in pursuit of reason and reasoning for human sorrows—"the problem of evil" and its theodicean responses (not to be confused with "grandiloquence"—the problem of pretentious authors using words such as theodicean and grandiloquence). Most often, this is no more than an exercise in futility.

Personally, I never asked why. Not because I wasn't curious, but because I already knew. Soon after I was diagnosed, I received an official document, outlining clearly and concisely the complex system of cause and effect that led to my present situation. The coveted information came in the form of a greeting card, sent by a "former" student. The front cover read: "Everything happens for a reason." The inside message explained: "Usually the reason is that life sucks."

So rest easy, great minds of moral philosophy and students of theodicy; ponder no more and fret not over the problem of good and evil. We've got it covered: it's all good. Except for the bad. But the bad is OK, too, so it's all good. Problem solved.

9
No Such Luck

Lady Luck and Lady Justice bump into each other one day.
Because one of them is blind and the other is blindfolded.

Almost Funny, p. 88

Everything depends on luck. Except for things that don't.
And everything else.

Constellations, Consultations, and Consolations 7:13

I should be grateful. I was lucky.

At least that's what they said. Most people who suffer from multiple myeloma are diagnosed when the condition is already at quite an advanced stage and serious symptoms are present—in a "good" case, after the persistence of severe back pain as a result of bone lesions and crumbling vertebrae, and in a bad case, after suffering from a pathological fracture—one that occurs "without adequate trauma," otherwise known by the charming name "spontaneous fracture" (a term which, incidentally, in a moment of loneliness, searching for a similarly unpopular match, might compose the following personal ad: "Fracture, spontaneous and open, straight hairline, overcoming recent breakup, seeking out-cast for support"). As the name would indicate, such an incident might appear quite out of the blue, rather than out of the black and blue, and an unknowing patient may thus be "informed" of his condition quite unexpectedly. Picture the scene: You're sitting at home one wintry day, nestled in a comfortable armchair, wrapped in a blanket of wool and

No Such Luck **45**

tranquility, blissfully ignorant of the inner workings of your skeletal structure. As you gaze dreamily out of the window at a peaceful world, you clasp a mug of steaming aromatic coffee in both hands, caressing it to absorb its heat. As your mind drifts, you raise the mug to your mouth, and your arm falls off. Or something like that.

But my diagnosis came about through a slower and more gradual process, without my body displaying any particularly alarming or painful symptoms. Lucky indeed.

Two things bother me about the all-too-common use of the phrase "you were lucky," or any other reference to luck: one—there's no such thing as luck; two—lucky people don't have cancer. And it's time to let these two things out of the box.

Thing one: Does anyone really believe in luck? *Can* anyone? What exactly do we even mean by this? To explain why things happen, there are two possible approaches: providence and chance. From a religious point of view, we believe that everything happens for a *reason*. God controls, or guides, every significant event. From a nonreligious perspective, there is not, and cannot be, a reason for anything. At best, and usually, there is a *cause*, or more likely a complex and progressive chain of many physical, chemical, biological, neurological, psychological, historical (and any other "ical" you can think of) causes and effects. Short of that, things are *random*, like the Brownian jiggling motion of dust particles in the air. Either way, there is no room for luck, whatever luck may be.

And what *could* "luck" be, if it were to be? It can't belong to the domain of nature, where everything either obeys fixed laws or no laws at all. So, it would have to be some sort of supernatural force. But it would have to be an unguided force, not controlled by a being executing a calculated plan; rather, it would be some sort of system that somehow manages to be spontaneous without being random. Or, in other words, nonsense.

I imagine that people who believe in luck, if anyone actually does and isn't just thoughtlessly using a meaningless term, are probably driven by the human propensity for self-centeredness and pattern seeking that intuitively drives us toward an explanation that places us in a system that somehow affects our lives, without being willing to take the next step of believing in an actual Divine being. Basically, depending on your starting point, luck is either blasphemy or irrationality, neither option particularly appealing.

Thing two: Putting aside the actual nonexistence of luck, applying it, even as a meaningless reference, to situations such as mine, makes little or no sense. Consider the following statement, and rate it from one to ridiculous: "You're lucky. You were diagnosed with a rare and incurable illness, in an age bracket that consists of a tiny percent of patients, early." Even if we were to give luck a chance, perhaps a lottery winner could be considered lucky (though probably not, in most cases). But in what possible way is someone lucky when he's shot in the chest and the bullet misses his heart by a quarter of an inch? Surely, he would be luckier had the bullet hit even farther away from the heart, and even luckier if the bullet had hit his shoulder instead of his chest, and luckier still if it had just grazed the skin of his shoulder, and very, very lucky if the bullet had missed him altogether. In truth, he would be really lucky not to be in a situation where he's being shot at in the first place, and luckier still if he was winning the lottery instead. So the bullet missing his heart by a quarter of an inch is in fact not very lucky at all, rather the least lucky scenario possible, short of being shot in the heart.

So why do we call him lucky? Because the bullet *was* flying toward the area of his heart, and within that *given* situation there were two possible outcomes, and since the one that did occur was the lesser of the two bad outcomes, he was lucky. But in fact he was not lucky at all; rather, he was merely not the worst possible version of unlucky. Not really much to boast about.

Which brings us back to thing one—providence and chance. If one believes that our victim was somehow placed in this situation and given the role of shooting target by way of conscious Divine decree, then we can start talking about the two options of being shot in the heart and being shot next to the heart as given options and define one as luckier than the other. However, if one believes in said Divine decree, one can no longer accept that the final outcome is subject to luck. For that, we would have to remove the initial axiom of being condemned to be shot in the chest area, leaving our victim a free man with extremely high chances of not being shot at altogether, rendering the almost fatal shot to the chest a nightmarish and very, very unlucky scenario indeed.

So much for good luck. And bad luck doesn't fare much better. When it comes to the question of why bad things happen, or "the question of evil," once again we have two possible approaches—religious and natural. In fact, one could say that there is really only one approach, though it is split into two totally opposite worldviews. The answer to the question "Why do bad things happen?" is that they don't. Bad things don't happen. For the believer, bad things don't happen because there is no "bad" in the world, only pleasant good and unpleasant good. In some way that is beyond the calculation and comprehension of us mortals, all things are good in the sense that they are part of God's greater plan, which is the ultimate good, suffering withstanding. For a nonbeliever, bad things don't happen either, or, to be precise, bad things don't happen any more frequently than would be expected according to the laws of nature and probability. For example, since there are only a handful of ways for the body to fully and painlessly function, and an infinite number of ways for it not to, no illness or physical suffering begs explanation.

So, believers and unbelievers alike, those who have reason to believe or those who believe only in reason, should shun the notion of luck and see it as an affront to both faith and rationality.

And, in any event, the whole question should be deemed irrelevant. Pondering on the "whys" of life is futile, since a believer believes that he can never really know with certainty why, and a nonbeliever believes with certainty that there is no why. All that there is, is what it is. And since what is, is, all that matters is what we do with it now.

And so, I make it my business to object to any reference to luck, in any shape or form. And though I am but one man and the task I undertake is great, I very much hope to be successful.

Who knows? I might just get lucky.

10
Taxi Returns

A clever man has a well-researched, clearly formed, and articulate opinion on every matter. A wise man knows how to shut up.

Sophie Kluger

You can learn a lot from taxi drivers. The vast repository of knowledge, unique brand of street wisdom, and deep insights they possess can be obtained only over a lifetime of observation and conversations with people of all walks of life.

And they talk a lot of rubbish, too.

As a freshly diagnosed cancer patient, I knew that I would be spending a significant amount of time in the hospital, both as a frequent visitor to the outpatient clinic and occasionally as an inpatient. What I didn't anticipate was that I would also be spending a significant amount of time in taxis. Returning from my first chemotherapy session, I bravely (i.e., foolishly) traveled home by bus (and light-rail, and another bus). As a seasoned public transportation patron, I didn't think it would be a big deal. But two hours of waiting, standing, sitting, boarding, alighting, front doors, back doors, and clinging on to a pole for dear life while standing on a swerving bus didn't do much for my physical well-being.

Of course, there was the hypothetical possibility of asking someone for their seat. But…that would be a different type of uncomfortable. How exactly does one go about such a request? "Excuse me, er, would you very much mind letting me take your seat, and you stand instead of me for an hour? The thing is, I have cancer, and I've just received chemotherapy. Yes, I know that I appear perfectly healthy. Yes, I am aware that I have hair. Yes, I am quite sure that I do indeed have cancer. No, I'm definitely not disrespecting real cancer patients and making light of a terrible illness just to get your seat. Whatever, thanks a lot, I'll manage. I can sit when? After you get off. Thanks. You're getting off when? I see, at the final stop. Very helpful, thank you. You're who? Oh, you're the driver. I'll let you get back to work, then. Thank you for your service."

And so, it was decided that taxis were the future of hospital return journeys.

I find taxi rides particularly uncomfortable, no matter how cushioned the seat. I'm never quite sure what the proper etiquette is, and what should be the interpersonal dynamic. It's a strange interaction, that of cab driver and passenger. You go, in no time at all, from complete strangers to sharing a very small space, for anything from a few minutes to what at times feels like forever. The moment you settle down in the passenger seat, you find yourself sitting close—closer than you would otherwise ever sit—to someone you've never met before, bound by your imminent joint journey. As a result, immediately, the "Cab-Ride Dilemma" strikes: To speak, or not to speak? That is the question.

In futile attempts to resolve this cringy conundrum, I've tried every possible form of cab conduct: sitting in the front seat in silence; sitting in the back seat in silence; sitting in the front seat pretending to be engaged in a very important phone call in which the required input on my side is a surprisingly minimal occasional "mm-hmm"; sitting in the front seat with headphones, listening to music; sitting in the front seat with headphones, pretending to listen to music; sitting in the front seat without headphones, pretending to listen to music; lying down on the backseats pretending to be asleep; lying down on the backseats pretending to be dead; sitting in the front seat with the window rolled down and my head out, pretending to be a dog.

After a while, with the passage of time, I ran out of ideas. And we were only halfway home. So I mustered up some artificial social might, looked the driver straight in the eye (well, technically I looked at the reflection of his eyes in the rearview mirror, but I'm sure there are some straight lines involved in the process of light bouncing between the sun, eyes, and mirrors), and said, "Hot day, ay?"

It turned out that I wasn't all that bad at small talk after all. Quite impressively, we managed to cover a variety of topics, such as the weather, the threat of nuclear war, and the weather. This newfound ability opened up a whole new world of cab-ride pastime possibilities. Now I could sit in the front seat and talk about the weather; sit in the back seat and talk about the weather; lie on the back seat and talk about the weather. I could even sit in the front seat and pretend to talk about the weather, and it wasn't awkward at all.

But I soon tired of the mind-numbing babble of casual human interaction that we are all slave to and progressed from meaningless coffee-machine small talk to massive talk. Within a mere few rides, I turned what was once an uncomfortably silent burden into a mobile therapy session, for no extra charge. At first, I approached the subject timidly, spending just a bit too long glancing at my arm and picking at the white sticky tape. "What, this? Oh, it's nothing, it's just the tape they put on when they removed the drip that they gave me BECAUSE I HAVE CANCER!" That would usually do the trick.

My subtlety skills soon deteriorated, and within a few days it was more like this: "Good afternoon, sir. Where to?"

"Home! And make it snappy, for I have cancer, and it is known that the patients of cancer must be delivered speedily to their destination, lest their condition worsen from the incessant chatter of laymen!"

Once the cancer can was opened, the taxi-ride experiences took on a whole new dimension—at times just dropping the bomb and at times following up with the aftermath of the destruction; at times sharing and at times listening; at times giving advice and at times taking it. All manner of cancer conversation ensued and accompanied the subsequent rides. Now I could sit in the front seat and talk about cancer; sit in the back seat and talk about cancer (lying on the back seat and talking about cancer didn't seem like the best idea); talk about cancer and hope for a profound insight; talk about cancer and hope for a profound discount.

All in all, over a period of two years I amassed an impressive number of travel conversations, and a no less impressive number of taxi drivers' calling cards, which are essentially numbers you should call if you want to wait longer than necessary for a cab.

All this brings us to the point—the wisdom behind the wheel. It was during one of these rides when, upon learning of my condition, this particular driver unhesitatingly responded with a confusingly compassionate gem of brainy brilliance: "Cancer? Ah, may God take all the cancer and throw it on the Xs" (read: racial reference, plural). In this short utterance, my solicitous chauffeur had captured, and generously shared with me, some of mankind's greatest "insights." Complex matters of philosophy, biology, sociology, ethics, and economics were all neatly folded into this concise statement. It revealed the following fascinating facts:

- There is a God.
- God cares about, and listens to, the plea of the simple man. No mediation, formal training, or donation is necessary.
- There is a predetermined and unalterable sum of cancer in the world. God can easily remove a portion of it from one individual without abiding by the restrictions of natural laws, but it must then immediately be introduced into the body of a different individual. In short, there is a law of conservation of cancer.
- It's not racism when you're the one being racist.
- It's OK to wish serious illness and death on people you've never met and know nothing about as long as they can be classified in some way or another. And they probably deserve it anyway because they were born.
- In a service-providing situation, it is mutually beneficial for both parties involved to still be alive at the end of the transaction, and therefore it is in a taxi driver's best interest that an unspecified and uninvolved third party be assigned the cancer in your stead so that he can collect his fee at the end of the ride.

All these extras, and he didn't even ask for a tip. Shame, I would have suggested a vow of science.

APPENDIX REGARDING TAXI DRIVERS

Readers of this chapter may have mistakenly gotten the impression that I have a hostile, or at least "interesting," attitude toward taxi drivers. This is not so. In taxi drivers I have found, over the years, many kind and wise individuals. Exactly like in every other profession. Naturally, I've also found some who are not so. Exactly like in every other profession. But I'm writing a book, not an advertisement for the ministry of transport, so forgive me for trying to make it somewhat interesting.

APPENDIX REGARDING THE APPENDIX REGARDING TAXI DRIVERS

Readers of the appendix regarding taxi drivers may have mistakenly gotten the impression that, really, I do have a problem with taxi drivers, and I wrote the appendix in order to cover myself in the event of criticism. This is not so. In taxi drivers I have found, over the years, truly decent, honest, and charming individuals. As a serial cab customer upon necessity, I have had the opportunity to meet a large number of drivers. As a serial cab customer traveling the same route routinely, I have had plenty of opportunities to ride with the same drivers multiple times. With several of them I have developed connections in varying levels of "closeness." In some cases, the connection is quite basic and amounts to me remembering the driver's name and he in turn remembering my address. In other cases, a more significant connection has been established, in which we both get to know each other to some degree, or at least get to know each other's medical issues and those of our families. In rare and cherished cases, a proper long-lasting relationship has developed, one that veers far off the beaten track and includes deep and meaningful talks and participation in family *simchahs*. Criticize that!

And yes, I know what you're thinking, and the answer is no, there will not be an appendix to the appendix about the appendix. You have reached your destination.

11
Take a Seat

If life gives you cancer, don't complain—some people never get anything.

Iffy Quotes, 1981

If life gives you lemons, ask life for some limes, carbonated water, sugar, citric acid, sodium citrate, sodium benzoate, high fructose corn syrup, caramel, and phosphoric acid, and make yourself a Sprite. Then throw it in life's face and say, "Enjoy this, life. I need something stronger."

More Iffy Quotes, 1978

In the living room of our humble abode, positioned unassumingly in a corner, we have a cancer chair. People are quite taken aback when they hear us refer to it as such. Needless to say, under no circumstances are they willing to sit in it, and they usually make a point of keeping a safe distance from it, placing themselves outside a radius that represents, apparently, the spreading limits of a non-infectious disease.

But the thing is that the cancer chair doesn't give you cancer. In fact, it's quite the opposite—cancer gives you the cancer chair. And this is how:

Soon after—though not particularly in relation to—my diagnosis, my wife decided to pursue a lifelong dream. "Life's too short," she said. The dream: owning a wicker chair. Reed, cane, bamboo, straw—any woven variety would do; the dream didn't specify the material, as long as it was wicker. Not necessarily of the garden variety, since our top-floor apartment wasn't furnished with one. A nice indoor one. Comfortable but elegant, soft but firm, light but sturdy. And wicker. Not so much a wicker-chair, really, but a wicker chair.

Why this wish had been so over-duly unfulfilled was unclear, but one thing was clear—now was the time to realize it.

It so happened that a family friend was in the vicinity of a furniture shop that day, and so, in she popped to see what treasures lurked within, in the wicker chair department. And there it was—a true throne of wicker, as coveted. In a flash, pictures were taken, pictures were sent, FaceTiming was commenced, and after brief deliberation, authorization was given: let it be written, let it be bought.

Priced at 350 (insert local currency for familiarity, adjust for realism), it was not unreasonable, albeit more expensive than all cheaper items and not buying anything. Before sealing the deal, the acquiring agent tested it out to make sure it was in good working condition, and to measure it for size and comfort. "It's for good friends of mine," she reported. "The husband was recently diagnosed with cancer, the wife could do with some cheering up, and a nice new comfortable chair would benefit them both." Apparently, I had cancer. Apparently, my wife needed cheering up. And apparently, the new chair would solve both problems. I guess you learn something new every day.

Upon hearing this, the chairman gave a thoughtful look, and after a moment said, "You can have it for 300. Here, let me help you carry it to the car." At the car, while lifting it into the boot, he gave an even more thoughtful look and said, "You know what, you can have it for free, with my best wishes to the family and blessings of health and comfortable sitting to the patient. Have a good day."

Soon thereafter, it arrived, in all its wicker glory, packaged with care, transported with love, and wrapped in freeness. And so it sits, quite humbly, in the corner of the living room, in no way betraying the secret drama that lies deep in its roots. We crowned it "the cancer chair," for obvious reasons. And for shock value, of course. Life's too short.

And till this day, people still don't get it. They don't understand the chair and what it stands for. People spend so much time and energy wondering about life's "why" questions, particularly when the question is "why bad things happen to me" (the other cosmic conundrum—"why good things happen to me" doesn't seem to inspire the same curiosity), while they should really be wondering and marveling at the gifts that every turn of life bears, even the ones that seem to be off course. But this is truly a shame. If we focus all our attention on the light at the end of the tunnel, we will surely fail to spot the treasures that lie in the dark.

People just don't get it. It's not the chair that gives you cancer. It's cancer that gives you the chair.

12
Leading the Poles

Life is like riding a bicycle. To keep your balance you must keep moving, or put your feet on the ground, or learn how to perform a track stand, or get training wheels, or any number of metaphorically meaningless possibilities.

Einstein's relatively not-so-special theory

Let's face it: sooner or later it was bound to happen. It was almost inevitable, one could say. Or at least so things seem now, when looking at the episode as reflected in life's rearview mirror—the only perspective that captures the scenery of human experiences with full clarity, unblurred by the fog of worry and doubt that limits the field of vision of the present moment.

Consider the facts: (1) It's an IV pole (2) on wheels. (3) It's an IV pole on wheels and I'm tied to it for hours and hours in a sitting room, with nothing to do. It was just a matter of time. At some point, I was going to ride the pole, and somewhere deep, dark, and wonderful inside, we all knew it, even if we didn't.

Boredom is a terrible thing. Terrible and wonderful. Wonderful because it's the unappreciated symptom of one of the most important attributes of our strange and amazing brains. Unlike other brained creatures, we humans are simply not able to just sit and do nothing. Those of us who have had the pleasure of raising teenagers may be inclined to dispute this statement, but that's just a question of how we define "nothing." Words mean different things to different people. For example, I just used the word "pleasure" in a way that probably sent some readers to a dictionary to make sure they still speak English.

In the animal kingdom, after a short period of play that mainly serves to prepare the young for being old, subjects are quite content with spending the rest of their lives doing nothing. Nothing, that is, other than what's necessary for survival, which in many cases takes up most or all of their time and includes everything. But other than that, their schedule consists almost exclusively of doing nothing, all the time. We, on the other hand, need constant stimulation. This wonderful phenomenon is what drives us to thinking, acting, developing, and inventing, and everything else that's of any value. Indeed, boredom is a wonderful and terrible thing. Wonderful because of all the wonders it spurs; terrible because it can drive you absolutely mad.

But what's really interesting is our capacity to become familiar with and adjust to new situations, even very unusual ones, and as a result find new opportunities to be bored. For the average person, words such as "cancer," "oncology ward," "injections," and "intravenous infusion" do not bring to mind, by way of association, the words "routine" and "boring." In fact, these words, to most, sound quite "special." But for long-term patients of a wide variety of illnesses, the experience of spending a day in the hospital, with all that accompanies it, very quickly becomes something very far from special, very much a routine, and as such, very boring. This is significantly compounded by the perhaps lesser-known fact that battling an illness, much like war, which has been described as "long periods of boredom punctuated by moments of sheer terror," consists mostly of waiting—before, during, and often after treatment, too, for good measure.

It was on one such mind-numbingly boring hospital day that our story took place. On that particular day I found myself soaring to new lows of boredom. In addition to my usual semiweekly treatment, I was receiving a bonus monthly treatment to prevent my bones from falling apart, not a particularly appealing prospect. Doubling up on treatments meant extending the stay at the hospital from very long to very, very long. After hours and hours of waiting, blood tests, more waiting, hooking up to a painfully-slow-dripping IV, more waiting, switching to another unhurried trickling IV, way too many cups of bad coffee and even worse cooking shows, I found myself at breaking point. Close to desperation, I listlessly rested my elbows on my knees, sunk my head into my hands, and stared at the floor and at the base of the IV pole that was on it. Suddenly, from some deep, strange, and wonderful place within me, an idea emerged, a thought that instantly turned into a decision, an absolute necessity, a Heavenly command. I have to ride the pole.

> *It starts tentatively, still sitting on a chair for inconspicuousness, gently testing the waters, just resting my feet on the rolling base-legs of the pole, lightly swaying to-and-fro. It progresses to a swivel, my lower body half-hovering in the air, arms stretched behind me tightly gripping the chair, in what can only be described as a circular dip-yoga-limbo motion. But then it's time to go full-on. Time to say goodbye to the chair and the familiar world it represented. I turn to my wife, who has not yet raised her eyes from the book she is reading, break the heavy silence, and say, "Push me." "What?" she responds, after finding me at the bottom of her field of vision. "No time for questions. I myself am not particularly sure what's going on. All I know is that you need to push me, as hard as you can, and as soon as possible, because for some reason the matter is both important and urgent." By this point I'm in full position, crouched down on the base, clinging to the pole for dear balance. And then comes the push, and away we go.*

To be honest, it wasn't exactly the thrill I was hoping for. My mental image of a top-speed, frictionless skid down the long ward corridor, saluting a speed-merged mass of dazed faces, was replaced by a reality obedient to the laws of gravity, friction, and air resistance. This was most disappointing (to me, that is. I imagine Newton's apple would have been quite proud). My journey amounted to a few feet of medium speed roll. But still, a roll it was. A roll that was followed by another—that of my wife's laughter.

But not everyone present at the performance was a fan. A nearby sitting bystander—a fellow patient waiting to see a doctor—was displeased by the sudden burst of motion and called out, "Are you drunk?" Was I drunk? Well, to be honest, I don't think so. Unless someone had spiked my saline with vodka, a generous gesture I certainly wouldn't object to (and would suggest naming "infused infusion"). But now that you've come to mention it, yes, I think I might have just been a little bit tipsy with a flicker of childish fun; perhaps somewhat intoxicated with a moment of being free of self-awareness; indeed, absolutely drunk with the refreshing realization that after seven long hours of being tied to a pole in the crowded waiting room of an outpatient oncology clinic, counting drip after impossibly slow-dripping drip of liquid that is somehow both poison and cure, it finally dawned on me that there are two ways to roll the wheels, and the question was this: Who's the boss? If I'm the star of the show, why am I schlepping the pole around? It should be working for me, getting me to my destination.

Sometimes life gives us a pole to carry. A pole weighed down by all sorts of fun-filled packages that loom above, dangling ominously—a variety of challenges, difficulties, and *tzaros*. And we are tied to these poles. They are the focal points of the circles of our lives, and everything we think, feel, say, and do revolves around them. But these poles come with wheels. And the choice is ours: Do we let them trail behind us heavily and grudgingly drag them along, or do we push them ahead with vitality? Do we succumb to these impositions and allow them to restrict our emotional space, or do we fight to break the boundaries they dictate? We can even climb these poles, reach new heights, find new perspectives, new *kochos*, and abilities we never knew we possessed. And, if we really want to, maybe, just perhaps, we can even ride the pole. Take it from me, it can be done. Just don't expect everyone around to understand you.

13
Hearty Donation

The test results have just arrived; it appears that your husband has a heart of gold. The bad news is that he is therefore, naturally, dead. The good news is that you're looking at a small fortune in precious metals."

Dr. Zahava Levtov

He who hates gifts will live. But without gifts, what kind of life is it anyway? And if I hate giving them, does that count?

Mishlei Emmett 15:27

This week I turned forty. Not something that happens every day. In fact, this is the first time it has happened to me, and I'm not exactly sure what the rules are. (There's definitely a "it's not my forte" joke somewhere in there, but I'm going to pass, we've all been through enough already.)

As a rule, in an attempt to view the world through rational lenses, I refuse to attribute any significance to (my own) birthdays, which are, if you think about it, just a day on which you are one day older than the previous day, something that can be said about quite a few other days throughout the year. In all honesty, is the fact that the oblate spheroid, on which we reside, completes its orbit around the giant and attractive yellow dwarf that stands in the center of the system that's situated on one of the six arms of our galaxy and finds itself almost in the same point in space in relation to it as it was 365.24 rotations ago a reason to feel significantly older than at any other given moment?

Apparently, it is. Despite the lack of correlation between the actual growth of our bodies and the relative positions of the celestial bodies to each other, we do indeed feel that years are cyclical, and consequently our birthdays, and other calendrically noted days, are special. It appears that a big impression is made on us by Earth's 23.5-degree incline in relation to the path it takes around the sun, a phenomenon known by some as "seasons."

Even if we put aside the technically insignificant timing of a birthday celebration, there seems to be a logical problem with the celebration itself. Traditionally, at least in most known cultures, the star of a birthday celebration is none other than the birthday boy himself.[1] The so-called "surprise" party, which for the sake of accuracy should really be called either a "shock" party or a "foreknown event in which the guest of honor must pretend to be surprised in order to satisfy the surprisers' need to surprise" party, is thrown for *him*, the gifts are bought for *him*, and the wishes are offered to *him*. But one could argue that the one person (or the twenty million who share his birthday) who doesn't have a reason to celebrate is the birthed one himself. By this I am not referring to the worn-out black pearl of dark "humor"—"You're one year closer to death," which (a) is not particularly funny, (b) would be true only if your moment of death was unalterably fixed and predetermined, and (c) is true at every given moment relative to one year prior to that moment. I'm getting at something much more fundamental, and potentially actually meaningful.

What exactly are we celebrating on a birthday? The arrival and continued existence of the aging individual. But the value of someone's existence, relative to the alternative of him not existing, can only be measured from the perspective of those who surround him, who could have, in theory, experienced a reality in which said someone doesn't exist. The sum of differences between these two possible realities, in

---

1 Legal clarification: as used herein, the masculine shall include the feminine as the circumstances may require.

the event that it's positive, is the cause for celebration. And this isn't applicable to the subject himself, since from his point of view, there's no meaning to the hypothetical alternative reality in which he doesn't exist, and consequentially no reference point for comparison. A world with pizza is objectively a better world to live in than a hypothetical and tragic pizza-less world, and therefore we have a reason to be happy to live in the world we live in (and anyone who begs to differ is welcome to prepare a full and detailed report outlining the arguments supporting their approach, post it into a dustbin/garbage can, and seek professional help). But a world in which we exist isn't, *for us*, a better world than one in which we don't exist, since in such a world there is no "us" that is worse off for it. So, even if there is a reason to party, the relevant party is not the birthday boy, but everyone else, and in principle they can do so without him (which would indeed introduce an element of surprise to the gathering), or at best invite him as a prop, together with the cake and decorations.

But thoughts and feelings, philosophy and human experience, don't necessarily go hand in hand, and even when they occasionally do, it's usually more of an arm wrestle than a friendly stroll. The reality is that arguments such as these don't matter. What does matter to people is birthdays. People feel something special on their special day, and that's that, and that's fine.

I figured that all the above notwithstanding, I should do something special to mark the milestone occasion. So I decided to give away my organs.[2] Then I remembered that I had cancer, and with that as a consideration, perhaps some people would be reluctant to claim my precious body parts. People are so picky these days. Though I myself am not totally free of this sentiment, either. Soon after my diagnosis, apropos of no prompting whatsoever, one particularly generous person offered me a kidney. "No thanks," I said. "I don't want a used one."

---

2   Religious clarification: the thoughts presented herein and henceforth are not intended as an expression of support, objection, or ambivalence toward any given halachic position regarding organ donation. They are presented, intended, and expressed as thoughts.

So I sent a message to my oncologist. "Doctor, Doctor, I was wondering, you know how I have cancer and all? Well, do you think I can still donate my organs?"

"Your organs? I'm not sure that's a good idea; I think you still need most of them."

"No, not now, after I die."

"Ah, I see. To be honest, I don't think they'll accept them; they won't want to take the risk. After all, your cancer is in your blood, and blood tends to travel around the body, visit the organs, and sometimes leave little gifts behind, too. The only things they might take are your corneas."

"My corneas? Oh, actually I wasn't thinking of giving those. You see, I tend to see the world in an 'interesting' light, and I'm not sure that my view of life is something that a hope-filled, optimistic eye-surgery patient would want to wake up to." I wasn't sure how he felt about that last comment, but I think the smiling-devil emoji that he sent in response was a sign of approval. As a rule, my approach to our relationship is that his job is to keep me alive, and my job is to keep him laughing. A fair deal, I would say.

I had never really given much thought to postmortem organ donation (postmortem of the donor, that is. I imagine that the reverse scenario would be quite pointless, and quite murderous), until one day I was struck by the sudden urge to prevent the terrible waste of precious body parts that could go toward saving and improving the lives of humans, instead of saving and improving the lives of worms. But now, as it turned out, it was too late. And the question I pondered was, what had I really wanted to hear: that I *could* donate my organs, or that I could not, or rather that I could *not*-donate them without guilt? And perhaps, what I really wanted was to want to donate them and be a better person than I really was. But wanting to want just isn't enough, no matter how much we want it to be.

As a teenager, I once gave blood. Once, and once only. The feeling of the needle wiggling inside my vein was so unpleasant that I never wanted to give blood again. Little did I know that twenty years later I would have needles in my veins left, right, and center, literally. Unfortunately, as so often is the case, this future experience didn't help much at the time.

Either way, my wish to avoid sharing my blood with others was soon granted to me, on account of some confirmed cases of bovine spongiform encephalopathy (pronounced: "mad cow disease"), a term that sounds much more like a Swedish death metal band than a medical condition. Not having had much contact with cows (though the same cannot be said about mads), I thought this was somewhat unwarranted, but such was the law of the land, and who was I to argue about cows when the safety of others was at stake. Apparently, this particular unwanted guest—the infecting agent—can lie dormant in its host for many years before bursting into action. So, even a short, long-ago visit to a potentially affected location, which is all I had to my discredit, can deem one unsuitable to be a blood donor. Henceforth, year after year, when all were summoned to give blood, I could stand pious and proud and proclaim, "Oh, how I would love to give blood; would it be that I could, I would give and give. Alas, the cows are mad; how sad, too bad." All it took to clean my conscious was a bit of unclean blood.

But that was then. What about now? Were my intentions sincere and the news received with a heavy heart, or was I secretly relieved to learn that my body would be of no use to others and that I could be buried in peace, in one piece? I'm not sure I can answer that question, and now that it's too late to test my sincerity all that remains is to wonder. Today, I look back in contempt at historical me, living all those years, thinking myself healthy and not initiating and arranging the future donation of my organs. How could he have been so selfish, so wasteful? But these surges of good surgical intentions are fruitless now. When I could, I didn't bother; now that I'm bothered, I can't. And present-day me, as righteous as he's trying to sound, can't really say with confidence that he would do things differently if given the chance. He's a big talker, but he can't put his body where his mouth is.

FROM THE HEART

It's a funny thing, organ donation. Not that I would know, but now that I didn't and I can't, the best I can do is muse over it. If you commit to giving your heart, are you expected to start taking better care of it from that point on? After all, what kind of person would you be if you gave a badly used heart? Heartless. It's probably safe to assume that the recipient won't be particularly pleased to hear that his new heart, on which he has placed his hopes, probably won't last that long and that he would be well advised to put himself straight back on the waiting list. Surely the right thing to do in such a case is to start following a rigorous exercise routine and do everything possible to keep the donation-to-be heart ticking on beat. But all aboard the irony train: would that really be fair? Such a lifestyle would surely extend one's lifespan, while the heart-transplant waiting list grew longer and longer, and the waiting patients grew more and more impatient. Hardly an honorable endeavor—jogging peacefully through a life of good health, while others, who need your heart just as much as you do, courteously die.

Perhaps, one would argue, it's not cardiac arrest or heart failure that we should be focusing on. After all, who wants a heart that already failed once? The more promising scenario (for the receiver, that is), is premature death (of the donor, that is)—an accident, perhaps. But the thing about accidents is that their outcome tends to be not particularly predictable. As such, hanging one's hopes on an accident that will render the body lifeless while sparing the heart, rendering it a spare heart, is a risky business. And so, the dilemma strikes again: on the one hand, as a committed and responsible donor, one would want to do one's best to prevent any possible trauma to the heart, and be dedicated to a hazard-free lifestyle, taking no or low risks. But of course, this would inevitably result in an increase in average heart-donor life expectancy, something which, as a whole, can't be particularly good for the industry.

So, there you have it, "The Donor's Dilemma" in all its gory glory.

The other thing about heart donation is that, well, to put it in simple terms, it's weird. The idea of your heart living on after you, and in someone else's body no less, is quite unnatural. "It is with profound sorrow that we announce the passing of...survived by his dear wife, beloved children, and his heart. If you'd like to pay a *shivah* call, they will be sitting in the family house. Alternatively, if you'd like to visit his heart, contact Steve."

Of course, by now we know that the heart is just a glorified pump, not the cradle of human emotion. But still, it's a heart. The thing that makes you alive. The symbol of essence. The heart of the matter. And it's mine. What in the world is it doing in someone else's body? Or perhaps the question is what in the world am *I* doing in someone else's body. What if I gave not just my heart but all my organs, my whole body for argument's sake? Only the brain would be his. Who would he be? Technically, he would still be him, just in a new (well, used) shell. Our body's cells are constantly replacing themselves as it is, so my present body isn't really my original one anyway; it's just a pretty good copy that looks a lot like the original.

But the brain is also part of the body, just a super-complex mass of matter. So who am I, then? When Scotty beams me up, all the atoms that compose me are taken apart, destroyed in some way, and then reassembled somewhere else, physically resembling the body and brain I occupied just a moment ago. But it's not really the same actual me. Basically, I've been killed, and a new me has been created. But somehow, everything non-physical about me is the same—the same memories, personality traits, and, generally speaking, the same "person." So what is the person? What is this abstract "mind"? Whatever it is, it appears that it is the real me, and I'm certainly not giving *that* to someone else. Well, if I did, it wouldn't be someone else, would it? It would be me in my new body. As it's been aptly put, in a brain transplant situation, you definitely want to be the donor, not the receiver.

Either way, for me it's a no-brainer. It's all in the mind for me, really, since I can't donate anyway. To be entirely honest, I'm actually quite relieved. I hate exercise.

APPENDIX

Not much point donating that, I guess.

14
Pains and Needles

Pain does a fine job of keeping us alive. It's just a shame that it has to hurt.

Painful Pondering

He who increases knowledge increases pain. Great news. Surely, then, my pains will be dull, few, and fleeting.

Scroll of Truths 1:18

It's not going to hurt this time. It can't possibly. How can it? It must be the hundredth time by now, and every time the pain is so brief that it's gone before it fully registers. By this point in time, I must be psychologically prepared so well that there's no way in the world it can actually hurt, is there? It's so definitely not going to hurt that this whole thought process must surely be a waste of time. Here it comes. And…yes, just as I thought, it hurt. That all-too-familiar micro-moment of sharp pain that represents the transition between impatiently waiting for the treatment to begin and impatiently waiting for it to end. A sensation that has accompanied me at every hospital visit throughout my journey, always keeping things fresh, and ensuring that every time we meet again is just as special and memorable as the first time.

Look away. No, look straight at it. Make a fist. No, let your arm lay limp. Think about something else. No, think about nothing else. Hold your breath. No, exhale slowly. Take it like a man. No, take it like someone who isn't a slave to gender-based stereotypes. Stop being a wimp. No, stop pretending not to be a wimp and just come to terms with the fact that it doesn't matter how many times you've done it; there's always that moment of fear-filled anticipation: *What will it feel like this time—will it sting?*

Don't get me wrong, I'm not afraid of needles. That would be unreasonable, irrational. Downright silly, to be honest. Needles don't bother me in the slightest. I just don't like them being shoved into my veins.

Is it a rational fear, a fear of something serious happening? Perhaps not. After all, what could really go wrong? Well, as it turns out, a few things. For example, it turns out that if you use the same vein for chemotherapy twice a week for a few weeks running, it can get infected and give all the impression of being a hard, sensitive, throbbing steel cable running down your arm. "Yes, that can happen," they said dismissively, after the fact. Thanks, good to know. Perhaps this fact should be included in the booklet of *Twenty Things You Should Know Now That You're a Cancer Patient*, right after "1. The clinic's coffee station is down the hall and to the left."

Or, for example, after enough tampering, your vein might explode, like the time I had an IV put in and taken out a few days in a row in a local clinic by a not-so-needle-savvy nurse who somehow managed to puncture my vein in a way that made it burst open under the skin, leaving me to watch in horror as a little blood-filled bubble appeared under the skin. "Oh," she said nonchalantly, "your vein has burst." Thanks, I thought, comforted to discover that at least she had completed the course "How to state the bleeding obvious" at the university of "you've been accepted; remind me again who you are?"

But, in all honesty, they're really not a big deal, needles. A bit of pain never hurt anyone. And the truth is that secretly (not anymore), strange as it may sound, I actually quite like the feeling of having a chemotherapeutic needle in my vein. There's something strangely soothing about it. Something about knowing that it's there, but at the same time not feeling it inside. Something about the way the skin goes cold as the fluid runs up the vein. Perhaps the comfort and safety of being treated, being connected to a source of healing, loathsome as it may be. If only we could find a way to get it there without going through the skin.

Despite the mostly tolerant attitude I developed toward needles, there was one particular needle I did have a small problem with: the one that was used to reintroduce my stem cells during my autologous bone marrow transplantation. It's not that I had something personal against it; I just had some difficulty understanding the geometry involved: how do you fit a needle into an arm when the needle is longer than the arm? OK, that might be a slight exaggeration, but it was definitely at least four inches long, give or take a few inches. There I was, thinking, in my naivete, that the fluid would be introduced through my PICC line, which was there, after all, for the introduction of fluids. But no, in comes a doctor brandishing what appeared to be a samurai sword. "You might feel some slight discomfort." You don't say. I made a mental note to buy him a dictionary as a token of appreciation for his kind services, and highlight the entries "might," "slight," and "discomfort." The task required the assistance of a nurse, who flattened out and stretched the skin on my forearm to accommodate the hollowed spike. As he was about to proceed, the doctor, who appeared to sense that I was in shock and couldn't believe that he was about to stab me with such a giant needle, perhaps because I said, "I'm in shock. I can't believe that you're about to stab me with such a giant needle," turned to me and said, "What, this little thing? It's actually the smallest needle from the big set. You should consider yourself lucky." Sure. I made another note to borrow his dictionary later and check if under "luck" there was any mention of shivers and a metallic taste at the back of the throat.

But, other than that, needles aren't that bad. In fact, they've taught me quite a few things, albeit mainly things about needles. Throughout my extended and various treatments, I have picked up all sorts of tips. This is what I've learned about needles:

- They're sharp.
- Given the choice, don't let a nurse or doctor put one in your elbow. Well, obviously never let them put one in your actual elbow, that would be weird, pointless, and needless to say, quite painful. I mean the elbow nook/crook/pit/interior/crease, the crelbow, or, as it's known informally, the "cubital fossa," the soft inner part of

your elbow where being stabbed with a needle really hurts. That's the one. It's a very convenient place to insert a needle. Convenient for them, that is. The skin there is thinner, and the vein fixed in place, making it easier to find and penetrate. A bit less convenient for you, however, if you plan on bending your arm at any point in the near future. It's all forearm and backhand for me. Medical staff may be less fond of that area, but I don't think the area is particularly offended—it's pretty thick-skinned. Granted, it does help if your veins resemble a bulging under-skin map of a city's water-pipe system.[1]

- The sting of having your skin punctured by one, signifying the start of the day's treatment, unpleasant as it is, is eclipsed by its counterpart—the mark of ending the session, i.e., removing the tape at the end. I'm not sure how I even have any arm hair, or arm for that matter, left at this point, but there seems to always be just enough to make sure that it hurts enough to make the same unjustified comment every time. During that always slightly uncomfortable moment, when a nurse has to stand just that bit too close for comfort and rip off the sticky tape, I find myself unable to resist the compulsion to make the same predictable comment, that wasn't even funny the first time: "Removing the tape is the worst part of the whole treatment, isn't it, ha ha." Seriously, they can put a man on the moon and a rover on Mars, but they can't invent needles that spontaneously appear inside veins and easily removable ultra-adhesive tape.

- No matter how many times you've had one inserted, that brief moment of dermal disruption when a needle is poked into you is still going to be unpleasant the next time. And no matter how much you think it's going to hurt this time, it probably won't be worse than last time, which you clearly survived.

---

[1] The above is not intended as a substitute for professional medical advice. It's meant as a substitute for misery.

The lesson? So many times in life, the fear is far worse than the feared, and we worry a great deal more than is warranted. Indeed, much of our fear in life (I'm truly sorry for this one…) is in vain.

A sharp point indeed.

15
Healthy, Wealthy, and Happy Ever After

Love heals. But so do most wounds.

A sign of good health

"Laughter is the best medicine." They say that, but I don't see people forgoing chemotherapy and taking clowning classes instead. I guess the sincere version—"Chemotherapy is the best medicine, but one should supplement the medical treatment with emotional care and cultivate general wellbeing, which can be greatly enhanced through laughter, since studies have shown that a positive outlook can have a significant impact on one's physical condition and might even help the treatment and the healing process itself"—just isn't as catchy.

The Seriously Incomplete Medical Encyclopedia

"The most important thing in life is health. I wish you good health."

Yes, thank you, and *Amen* to that. Succinct. Original. I've never heard that one before. Except, of course, for every conversation I've had in the last three years, especially the brief and inconsequential courtesy ones conducted within the walls and halls of the hospital.

It's not that I don't understand where it comes from. After all, here we are sitting in a room full of extremely sick people—sorry, "patients"—strapped to bags of liquid life, one wearing a face mask, another sporting a bald head, a third slouched limply in a wheelchair, and another lying in a bed, curled up in the fetal position, groaning. What blessing are we going to bestow upon each other if not the good old "the most important thing is that you should be healthy" gem? I understand. It's justified, it's nice, and it comes from sincere kindheartedness. It's all those things, and more. But is it true? This is a question that we appear to rarely ask ourselves in general, and certainly not when it comes to big statements that assert with confidence that "the most important thing in X is Y."

If one were really in the mood to pick apart this kind of all-encompassing statement, even before examining the specific Y that is being championed in any particular such assertion, one could question what exactly is meant by positing that it's "the most important thing" in X. Do we mean "a factor that is greater in importance than any other one factor," or "a factor that is greater in importance than all other factors combined," or "a factor without which the value of all other factors is diminished," or just "something *really* important"? But even if for the moment we can forgive the ambiguity that is so typical of inflated statements, when it comes to this particular example we needn't be so accepting of its claim to certainty.

Perhaps it's time to start a revolution and propose a new candidate for the position of "most important." And perhaps, even before that, we should put forward a motion to dismiss the entire endeavor of deciding for other people what the most important thing is and/or should be for them. I, for myself, believe in a different "the most important." In truth, my formulation is uncannily close to the popular version. I think that "the most important thing in life is *not* health." Not that I have something against health (though, as it appears, my body has its own opinion about that one). Rather, I believe that focusing exclusively on the importance of health is itself somewhat of an illness. I'm sure that if we tried hard enough, we could probably come up with a definition that includes both, something like "a health-related condition that limits one's ability to enjoy life." But let's not invest too much time on such an unimportant detail; that would be unhealthy.

My problem with "the most important thing in life is health; I wish you good health," has two parts—one for each part of the statement:

The first issue is a bit technical and somewhat nitpicky, but no need to thank me—that's what I'm here for. Putting aside the philosophical side of things and focusing purely on the practical wishy aspect, we have an issue here. "You should be healthy." "I wish you good health." What do you want from me? I have a chronic disease. There's only going to be one future point when the illness will be gone, and at that point health will be the least of my concerns. If, for example's sake, we were to bump into each other and I had pneumonia (as I happen to have while writing these lines), by all means, wish me good health, i.e., that with proper treatment the infection will clear up, my health will be restored, and I will subsequently be pneumonia-free. Your wishes would receive a warm, even feverish, welcome. But when we're dealing with a condition that's considered incurable, in order for the blessing "you should be healthy" to be in any way meaningful we would have to suggest creative interpretations, such as "I hope you don't contract some other illness, and thus, with your one chronic illness, you'll be healthy relative to the multitude of other available illnesses." Or "I hope a miracle happens and the otherwise uncurable condition that you will be in and out of treatment for, for the rest of your life, will be cured." Or "I hope that the active periods of your chronic condition will be as spaced out and as pleasant as possible within the limits of what is realistic to expect, and that during those periods of treatment your experience will be as tolerable as possible under such conditions." Personally, that last one is my favorite version, and when people ask if I would be comfortable with them davening for me, that's what I ask them to have in mind.

The second issue is that the above—the practical aspect of wishing a growth out—is really just an outgrowth of the main question of what indeed is "the most important thing in life." This is the million-dollar question, a phrase that, incidentally, already reveals something about our priorities in life. I wonder if there's a remote people somewhere out there in which the phrase is the "two-years-of-good-health-and-a-semi-functional-family question" or has a game show called *Who Wants to Be a Healthy Person with 2.4 Children and a Dog?* I'll leave that one for anthropologists.

Here, too, I believe, matters are not so simple. I'm inclined to say that "the most important thing in life is not health." Not always. Granted, when someone is in excruciating pain, when someone's quality of life is so low that there's just no room left for anything else, then yes, the most important thing is to be healthy or, to be precise, less ill. But in that sense, we might as well be saying that the most important thing in life is being alive, because if you're not alive then it's quite hard to have a good life. But for us average illness-inflicted patients, the ones who are, on the whole, living a normal life of sorts, facing challenges, discomfort, various degrees of treatment, and all the experiences of long-term illness, health is not the most important thing. Something else is.

I imagine that at this point, some readers are anticipating something along the lines of the following: "The most important thing in life is not health; it's the other 'h'—happiness." Don't worry, that's not exactly where I'm going with this, but it's not too far from it, either. An interesting experiment to conduct is to type "the most important thing in life is h" into Google and see if the autofill prediction is "health" or "happiness," and then to wonder how it was determined. Is it based on popular search, your personal settings, your search history, or information Google has been collecting about you in order to advertise health/happiness products to you? Or perhaps the all-knowing Google is actually telling us the true answer to this question.

This is usually where the corny, syrupy, sticky, sweet part comes in about the importance of *simchas ha'chayim*, good relationships, and a sense of purpose. Then comes the part about marveling at the breathtaking beauty of a cloudless and vibrant blue sky that stretches as far as the eye can see, touching a glistening and endless field of wheat, as a magnificently orange sun gently sinks beneath the horizon. Or is it rising? It's hard to tell in many of these images.

But don't worry, that part isn't coming, not in this chapter, or book, or any book written by this author, for that matter. I'm not the right address for that delivery. My standards are much lower. All I require is to be able to, when appropriate, laugh life in the face. To not take myself, or anything that happens to me, too seriously. To know how to shift the focus from the unbearable to the unbreakable. OK, so I was up all night, tossing, turning, moaning, and mainly vomiting, and now I feel too weak to get out of bed. OK, so I feel nauseous, and I don't know if it's the regular kind when the last thing you want to do is eat, or the special cancery one when all you need to do is eat to make it better.[1] So what? Does that mean that life is all bad? Is this attitude, which allows me to find some peace and pleasure in everything, less important than health, which is entirely out of my control, and certainly not a guarantee of happiness? At the end of the day, it all boils down to one principle: our ability to respond to life is our responsibility.

"You should be healthy." There's one more problem with that blessing. I'm fed up with people telling me that "things will be OK." Things *will* be OK? No thank you. That's not enough for me. Things *are* OK; things are OK *now*, even when they're not. I can't afford to spend my life waiting for the bad to exit left and good to take center stage. And why should I, when good and bad can play together in the sun, even if the mood is somewhat dampened by pain's reign?

So don't wish me health; wish me happiness. I'll take happiness over health any day. Actually, I'll take them both if you're offering. But apparently, you're not, so I'll settle for happiness. That way I can enjoy what health I do have, instead of suffering through a miserable life of full health.

---

[1] The above should not be taken as professional medical advice. Before acting always consult your local stomach.

16

Impatient Inpatient

Hospital [noun]—the first place you ever see, and the last place you ever want to see again.

The Complete Dictionary of Incomplete Truths

I'm a big believer in either doing something well or not doing it at all (I refrain from using the popular version "go big or go home" because the second option would always be more appealing to me, and I would never get anything done). Always pursue perfection. Or, to put it slightly less glamorously, embrace your strengths and run from your weaknesses. This dubious approach was well reflected in my high school report cards, which were always strange mosaics of excellence and failure. As it turned out, my health was no exception to this polarized pattern. In my wife's words, "You couldn't just catch a cold or something, could you? You had to go and get yourself cancer. Classic."

In the years BC (Before Cancer), I had never been in the hospital on account of my own health or lack thereof. I was, however, no stranger to hospitals, not by any stretch of the imagination. My kids had provided me with plenty of hospital-visiting opportunities. Putting aside the birth-related trips, for which they perhaps merit some degree of absolution, they offered a seemingly inexhaustible supply of causes for us to pay the occasional emergency room visit, more often than not due to somewhat interesting incidents.

On one such occasion, my boys were playing tag in a playground, and my then-five-year-old, apparently confusing "tag" for "push very hard," shoved my then-four-year-old off an eight-foot slide, sending him gliding not so gently toward the not-so-soft ground. Surprisingly, upon superficial inspection, he seemed fine. But when the local doctor asked, "Does his nose always look like that?" we realized it might be a bit more serious than we'd thought. "No, his nose doesn't always look like that. It's not usually three times bigger than it usually is." He had "swollen" written all over his face. So we made the trip to the emergency room, where we were relieved to find out that it was just a mild case of severe pain. There was no damage, and no treatment was required. Following the incident, the playground was given a makeover and a new slide was installed. To this day my son is convinced that the recent modernization of playgrounds countrywide, in which the old, rusty equipment, sand, and gravel have been replaced with safer equipment and rubber mulch flooring, is entirely due to his incident.

Not long after the first episode, the same son, now a six-year-old, fell victim to a Playmobil-related incident. You can't be too careful with toys that contain small parts, choking hazard and all, and it's jolly good of the manufacturers to attach the appropriate warning labels, which usually read something along the lines of "Warning: contains small parts and traces of peanuts. Not suitable for children under the age of twenty-five. And don't forget to cut their sausages this way and not the other way." But as it turns out, even the most detailed cautionary counsel can't guarantee complete safety. Nowhere, not even in the small print, does it say, "Beware: your older brother will ram this figure into your head. You will bleed. You will need stitches. You will have a scar that will show when you get a short haircut."

And this wasn't the only case of battery that my son was involved in, landing us in the emergency room. Lists of "ten most dangerous things pediatricians say you shouldn't have in the house" usually include trampolines and watch batteries, those small silver coin/disc/button-shaped ones that usually come in cheap toys, the kind that often come pre-broken in order to save everyone the time and effort. Regarding the batteries, I'm willing to concede. I'm still on the fence about the trampolines, at least until someone reports a case of a child shoving one up his nose.

Is there anything cuter than a four-year-old boy sitting on a floor, staring with wonder at an electric musical dreidel bouncing, bobbing, and spinning around, playing Chanukah songs and shining colorful lights in every direction? Probably. But there are definitely plenty of things that are less cute, such as that same child bursting into your room and announcing, "The good news is that the dreidel is broken, and you don't have to listen to that irritating noise anymore. The bad news is that I've shoved one of the batteries up my nose and I can't get it out."

A cursory glance, which revealed nothing, suggested that the battery must have been inserted quite deep indeed, so much so that we had serious concerns that if we didn't act swiftly, he might turn into the Energizer Bunny. Even our longest pair of tweezers was no match for his nasal passages. We rushed to a local medical emergency center, where a doctor used the latest state-of-the-art medical equipment—the flashlight on his phone—to peer into my son's nose. Upon inspection he reported confidently, "It's definitely not there. It must have fallen out. You can go home." Something must have been lost in translation, perhaps due to our own confidence that we would have noticed such a thing, and what we heard was, "It's definitely there. It hasn't fallen out. Go to the hospital." I rushed to the emergency room, where I was greeted by an ENT who shared the delightful prognosis: since the battery was lodged so far up his nose, and since the battery was a battery, immediate action needed to be taken lest the acid in the battery start dissolving and damage his eye. She said she would have one go at trying to remove it before rushing him into surgery. Aided by a randomly selected strapping young lad, I held down his small and wildly struggling body while the doctor, using an even brighter light and an even longer pair of tweezers, successfully retrieved the battery. Once removed, he fell still immediately, drained of energy.

A week later, there was a small article in a local paper, headlined "Parents beware: small batteries health hazard," followed by a short description of our little incident and an X-ray of my son's head, with a red arrow pointing to the top of his nose. I have no idea who wrote the piece, how they got the information, and most of all how they got hold of the X-ray. I suspect it was an image of some random person's head pulled out of an archive (a procedure that itself probably requires a follow-up X-ray) for the benefit of those who might not know exactly where in the face region one's nose is located.

I learned a few things from this experience, but one thing above all. I think it's safe to say that there is a very short list of things you should push up your nose, and, as always—batteries not included.

Emergency rooms are, no doubt, not the most hospitable places in the world. Fair enough, they can hardly be expected to provide a relaxing vacation experience. But there's one thing in particular about them that I really can't stand. "999/911/112/000/111/101 [insert local number here if I missed yours], what's your emergency?"

"Please, somebody, help me!"

"Sir, are you in an emergency?"

"Yes, I'm in an emergency. Room. I'm in an emergency room, and somebody's taken all the chairs! There are no chairs, anywhere! I repeat: no chairs. Please, oh please, God, somebody help me. They've given my son a bed, but I'm just pacing up and down the corridor, and there are no chairs anywhere in sight. Oh, I've found them. I've found the chairs. Panic over. They're in the next cubicle. All the chairs are in the next cubicle. There seems to be some sort of family event taking place there—there's food and drink and people and a guy bleeding to death in the corner, and chairs everywhere. Emergency over and out."

So yes, I've been to the hospital a fair share of times, and those were just a few of our visits, following one particular child's injury résumé, and the other kids don't fall far behind. But throughout all these visits I was merely a visitor.

Naturally, with the transition to AD (After Diagnosis), this all changed. When I suddenly found myself on the other side of healthy, and the hospital beds were turned, the environment was familiar but the feelings that filled it were foreign. It doesn't matter how many times you've been to the hospital with someone else; nothing can prepare you for the experience of being hospitalized yourself. Nothing can prepare you for just how much *better* it is. I always thought that hospitals just weren't my thing, that I was ill-equipped to deal with them. But as it turned out, although I was a lousy carer, probably due to my being extremely impatient, hidden inside all along was an amazing inpatient. I was just very well suited for the position. I don't mean in the Munchausen sense. I just function very well propped up in a bed, reading, snacking, and doing pretty much nothing else. Granted, at first, some adjusting was necessary: the bed had to be adjusted and set to the right angles, not before testing its limits and raising it to its full four-foot potential, of course. (I try to avoid using the official product name—"electric bed"—since it sounds not so much like a piece of hospital furniture and rather a lot like an ever-so-slightly more comfortable and improved version of the traditional execution apparatus.) The chairs had to be positioned strategically to provide maximal viewing options in relation to the wall-mounted screen, and some of the kids' drawings had to be put up as a small reminder of their absence and the peace and quiet that came without them.

I also brought with me a guitar and a ukulele. I didn't plan on playing much, but I felt that it would create a softer, more homey atmosphere (assuming that one's home features a guitar and a ukulele). Music is one of life's constants. Through all its ups and downs, right and wrong turnings, it's always there; we just have to open our ears and hear it. As an anonymous sticker once read, "Music is the flowers on our handcuffs."

This instrumental presence led to some interesting situations. On my first day in the bone marrow transplantation ward, a welcoming party of hematologists, immunologists, doctors, professors, and interns entered my room, semi-circling my bed, which I thought was a bit strange considering that I wasn't in it at the time. In order to keep with the time-honored hospital tradition and follow the established custom, I took my position as *"nebach* in a bed," and they started briefing me about what to expect throughout the forthcoming four weeks. Before getting very far, one of the doctors noticed the small, triangular cardboard box on the bed, and inquired as to its contents. In way of answering, I whipped out the ukulele. On key, much to everyone's surprise, the inquisitive middle-aged doctor—whom the others referred to as "Igor," presumably because his name was Igor—grabbed the small instrument and started playing, quite skillfully. As he strummed and plucked, his features melted with dreamy nostalgia, while the straight-faced ensemble of experts looked on in a blend of amusement and impatience. "Perhaps, with your permission, Doctor," one of them finally spoke, addressing him as one would a misbehaving child, "we could continue?" The meeting went smoothly after that.

Two weeks later, another rhythmic rendezvous took place. After adjusting, or replacing, or refilling, or injecting Red Bull, or whatever it is nurses do to one's IV every few hours, this particular nurse sat down heavily on one of the chairs in my room. An unoccupied hospital nurse is somewhat of a rare commodity, and until that moment I had never seen one sitting and was quite unaware that they bend at the knees. I suddenly found myself on foreign social territory. Unsure as to the proper conduct in such a situation, I did what I do best—nothing, stealing the occasional glance at the dripping of my drip in a failed attempt to divert attention away from the overbearing silence. At last, she spoke. She said, "I hope you don't mind; I just need a few minutes of peace and quiet. All the other patients are so demanding—'Can I have a sip of water to wet my dry, cracking lips; can I have something to ease this pain, to relieve that suffering; my oxygen mask has slipped off; can you save my life, blah blah blah,'—they just don't stop." Then she insisted that I play a song. "Come on, I'm not leaving until you play something for me on the guitar." Um, "Things Can Only Get Better"? With little choice, I strummed a few chords and twanged a few strings. I didn't sing, though. Bald and sporting ill-fitting hospital pajamas I may be, I mused, but I still have some self-respect left. Well, perhaps not. But I'm not singing.

Given the choice to spend a month away from home, anywhere in the world, would a hospital room be my first-choice booking? Probably not. But that didn't stop me from trying to celebrate my little cell as much as I could. We rarely get to tailor-make our circumstances, but we can certainly decorate them. You'd be surprised what a difference a couple of musical instruments, some pictures on the wall, a jigsaw puzzle, a smile, a pile of unread books, and a funny mug can make to a hospital room. And to life.

17
Ice, Ice Maybe

Physicists will tell you that dark is just the absence of light, cold is merely the absence of heat, and science as a whole is nothing but the absence of blind faith. Precisely the sort of definitions I would expect from absence-of-light-minded, absence-of-heat-hearted absence-of-faith-ists.

I.C. Treats

In the category of "worst thing to happen to me over the past few years," the nominees are:

1. Having cancer
2. A kidney biopsy
3. Five days of internal bleeding
4. A bone marrow biopsy
5. Six months of injections to the stomach
6. A year and a half of chemotherapy and steroids
7. Mood swings
8. Insomnia
9. Stomach cramps
10. Nausea
11. Enough pills to make me rattle
12. Having a PICC line inserted
13. A bone marrow transplantation
14. A month in isolation
15. Hair loss

16. Another bone marrow biopsy, through the chest
17. Total exhaustion
18. Hundreds of needle pricks
19. Twenty other flavors of torment and suffering

And the award goes to…a mouthful of ice!

Yes, that's what did me in, a mouthful of ice. Well, to be honest, not just one mouthful—three continuous hours' worth of mouthfuls of ice.

The particular variety of poison-therapy that was administered in conjunction with my bone marrow transplantation is notorious for causing damage to the digestive system, all the way from one end to the other, pardon my *anatomique explicite*. In advance of the pain and discomfort, several precautions were taken, most of them in various forms of the warning "These following weeks are going to be terrible for you." Thanks. Articulate and comforting. One particular more specific and preventive measure involved ice. In order to minimize the flow of harmful chemicals to the mouth area, and by doing so reduce the number and intensity of mouth sores, the medical staff warmly recommended that I suck on ice throughout the two-hour procedure and the hour that followed it. Crunching the ice between my teeth was an option, too, but that was really biting cold.

The notion that a mouthful of ice could be on par with any one of the above-listed afflictions, let alone surpass the total sum of their induced suffering, must sound absurd. But trust me: this is a trick the Spanish Inquisition missed, one that counter-terrorist "enhanced interrogation technique" policymakers may still want to consider adopting, and a plague whose full potential Moshe Rabbeinu only slightly overlooked.

But how bad can it really be? After all, we've all had ice lollies/ice-pops/ices/popsicles, or whatever the local term is for our favorite water-based ice snack. Most of us probably don't remember it being particularly intolerable, and generally speaking, it appears that the ice-treat market supports a stable and growing industry that can be traced all the way back to the invention of cold.

But, as so often is the case regarding health, pleasure, and a multitude of other matters, the key is moderation. Even too much water and oxygen can kill you, provided that they get some help reaching you. A mouthful of ice, flavored or otherwise, is tolerable if not pleasant. Three unending hours of it are torture.

To be honest, though, the real-time experience itself wasn't the main issue. Granted, three long hours of extreme discomfort due to overstimulated thermoreceptors are no walk in the park, unless the park is located in the ghostly and lifeless remains of a post-apocalyptic frozen earth. But these excruciatingly slow flowing hours were in truth nothing but a countdown to the grand launch of a greater, unexpected, and longer-lasting form of misery that can be dubbed PITGAD—post ice-trauma gag disorder. The condition, simply put, can be described as follows: any interaction with ice or any ice-related substance, including tasting, touching, seeing, and being in the presence of ice, triggers a violent gag reflex and the uncontrollable urge to vomit. Conventional medicine, as it stands today, offers only one course of treatment for this condition: stay away from ice. The problem is that studies have effectively shown that in most large cities, at any given time, one is never farther than an average distance of zero centimeters from one's head. And one's head, which traditionally houses one's brain, memory, and imagination, is where all the ice in the world takes permanent residence under the influence of this particular condition. It's very hard to escape from yourself. Even if, by some supernatural feat, you do manage, you'll probably find yourself waiting for you at your destination.

The full intensity of the issue became evident to me quite soon after the initial trauma. That very same day, the aggressive chemotherapy I had been administered already started taking effect, and I was experiencing some serious nausea. I'm not sure if "serious" is an official measure of degree of nausea, or if its counterpart adjective "jokey" is in popular use in this particular context, for that matter. In fact, I'm not all that sure that there is an official nausea scale, and if there was, what units of measure it would use. "Good morning, how are you feeling today? I see. And how would you rate your nausea, on a scale of 'Ooh, I think I overdid it a bit with that second burger' to 'Ooh, I think I've just inhaled the moderately decomposed carcass of a diseased rat'? A few degrees north of 'violent viral gastroenteritis,' you say? OK, then, take some of this 'drug that does absolutely nothing'; it usually does its job."

Officially rated or not, serious nausea is what I was experiencing. Amid this tournament of torment, a nurse came by to do whatever it is that nurses do, which—judging by their omnipresence and doctors' omni-absence—appears to be absolutely everything except for signing the piece of paper that says, "Give him some more of that drug we gave him the other day; perhaps this time it will work," a power reserved only for the highest ranking and most evasive members of staff.[1] Upon inquiring, and noticing that I was green, she noted my nausea and kindly informed me, with the excited tone of one who is about to profoundly change your life for the better, that many patients say that the most effective way to relieve nausea is...sucking on ice.

She was dead serious. I felt much closer to the former than the latter. Ironically, it worked, albeit not exactly in the way she had in mind. The mere mention of the wretched substance did in fact bring immediate relief to my nausea. That's generally what happens when you vomit, the most, and perhaps only, effective method of relieving nausea known to mankind.

This newfound trauma was no short-lasting matter. Months later, the question "Would you like to go out for ice cream?" would still be enough to cause a deeply unpleasant sensation of revulsion. Even free of triggering, icy thoughts would pop into my head and cause all sorts of nauseous havoc. At the time, I was still receiving a motley crew of treatments, including chemotherapy and steroids, side effects included, and still the freezy frenzy was my greatest tormentor. Something had to be done. Uncharacteristically, I sought professional help.

I'm not sure how many psychiatrists/psychologists/therapists/bartenders/high priests/witch doctors throughout the history of emotional care have been approached with such a complaint, but there seem to

---

[1] The above is not intended to express disrespect toward doctors or cast doubt on the busy schedule they keep. I'm sure they work tirelessly, day and night alike, serving the public. This can be verified easily and in a satisfactory manner. All we need to do is find them.

have been enough patients with a similar condition for someone to coin the term "pagotophobia," the fear of ice cream, which is (apparently) the fear of getting frozen in the mouth, or the body freezing from the inside, not to be confused with pagophobia, the fear of ice and frost, which is a fear of slipping on ice and getting injured. (On a related note, I sincerely believe that the vast number of bizarre "official" phobia names that have relatively recently surfaced from the depths of language are entirely the brainchild of a highly prolific individual suffering profoundly from a type of phobophobia, specifically, a fear of unnamed fears. Personally, those sorts of people scare me. Good luck finding a name for that one.)

Either way, I sat opposite the psychologist and prepared myself to share. I have to admit, I was a bit uncomfortable bringing up my glacial malady, in all its pathologically pathetic-sounding splendor, especially considering the fact that I was about to pitch it as an affliction more dreadful than the cancer that brought it about. I think he sensed my sensitivity, because the first thing he said was, "Should we perhaps start with some small talk, to break the ice?"

Five minutes, some wet wipes, and a new carpet later, we settled down and began deliberating my debilitating frosty fear, and possible strategies for overcoming it. It was quite simple, really; battling a fear of ice boiled down to one thing: exposure. Bit by bitter-cold bit, step by brisk step, in increasing levels of closeness, I would have to engage with ice, until fully desensitized. And so, I did. This isn't my log from those drizzly days:

- Day one: thought about ice; felt sick.
- Day two: tried very hard not to think about ice; felt sick.
- Day three: felt sick.
- Day seven: wondered where the last three days went; felt sick.
- Day eight: opened the freezer door, stood paralyzed in a cloud of vapor; felt sick.
- Day eleven: started getting used to freezer vapor; felt a bit light-headed from four days of standing.
- Day fifteen: opened the freezer door, touched frost; felt sick. And cold.

- Day twenty: bought a slushy; felt slushy.
- Day twenty-one: bought a slushy and took a sip; felt a bit less sick than I expected.
- Day thirty: started thinking I needed a more interesting hobby.
- Day three-years-later: this is more or less where things stand now. I can handle almost any ice-related rendezvous short of actually having ice cubes in my mouth, something I think I just might be able to live without.

Along my icy adventure, I learned several things, of varying levels of insignificance. But above all I learned what I believe is a simple and unfortunately unappreciated fact: the greatest pleasure in life is merely the absence of pain.

18
Unhappy Feet

I'm a firm believer in alternative medicine, so long as the medicine that it's an alternative to is alternative medicine.

Dr. Alter Nater

Veni, vidi. Vici? Not so much. I came, I saw, and then I backed up slowly and quietly without anybody noticing, turned around, and ran, because I'm really not good at confrontations.

Chicken Caesar

You can do this. Just look away. Perhaps close your eyes and try to think about something else, somewhere else, some-when else. Nothing to see here! Nothing out of the ordinary! Just a random guy you met two minutes ago rubbing oils and massaging your feet. Yep. Not awkward at all. Nothing noteworthy is afoot.

It's a few days after the bone marrow transplantation, and I'm lying in my hospital bed, just another mind-bogglingly boring day in a lonely world, and in walks a man. "Hello, my name is X (where do they get these weird modern names from?), and I'm the ward reflexologist. You may not be aware, but it's a well-known and documented fact, supported by extensive research conducted by 'the institute for foot-rubbing and crackpottery,' that in seven out of six cases, a foot massage can cure cancer. Unless you have cancer. In that case you'll just be experiencing unwanted and unwarranted hand-foot contact with a stranger.

"So, let's not waste any time. I'll just snap on these blue rubber gloves to create a kitchen-drain-cleaning atmosphere and get straight to work. We'll start by opening this suspicious looking tub of Vaseline-like muck, in no way contaminated by years' worth of bacteria, dead skin, and vintage fungus from the feet of every cancer patient in the history of modern medicine. This may feel a little warm, either due to a chemical reaction, or the profuse sweating that accompanies the overstepping of one's foot privacy boundaries.

"And now for the rubbing. You just lie back and relax, and I'll go on with the treatment, and make small talk to guarantee maximum uncomfortableness throughout the duration of the experience. So, where are you from?"

"Oh, me, I'm from a small town called AAAGGGHHH-THIS-IS-SO-AWKWARD-GET-ME-OUT-OF-HERE-ville. It's a few miles south of highway mad-crazy-ill-at-ease. You may know it; people there are known for being quite sensitive to absolutely abnormal interpersonal interaction."

Quick, think, where do I look? Do I look at him? Where's he looking? At my feet. OK, so I'm looking at him and he's looking at my feet. And what about my feet? Oh no, this is not good, my feet are looking at me! It's a triangle of awkwardness—there's no way out! OK, I know—I'll look at my feet. Then it's all good—everyone's looking at my feet. But now he's looking at me. *Stop looking at your feet and have a conversation like a normal person*, I chastise myself. Well, a normal person who's having his feet massaged without being given sufficient time for mental preparation.

Now, here's the problem. This foot-massage business, it's *really* enjoyable, deeply pleasurable. Do I believe that the sole of the foot is a microcosmic map of the entire body's nervous system? No, I think it's just a very sensitive surface that contains a vast number of nerve ends that assist bipedal balance. But who knows? Maybe it does work. Legend has it that Danish physicist Niels Bohr kept a horseshoe above his desk. When asked by a surprised visitor how a man of science such as himself could believe in such a superstition, he responded, "I understand it brings you luck whether you believe in it or not."[1] Perhaps foot massages are the same. And perhaps not. But all that is beside the point. The point is that it feels amazing. And that's the problem. A foot massage is exactly the kind of experience you don't want to undergo with a stranger present.

In the end, I decided to just let him get on with it. Basically, I didn't want to upset him. Selfless serving of others is a key feature of the hospital environment, and this was my little contribution. Indeed, a truly courageous feat.[2]

---

[1] Whether or not the story is correctly attributed to him, if the horseshoe was hanging above his desk or above his doorway, and to what extent this quip contributed to him winning the Nobel Prize in 1922, remain open questions.

[2] The above is not intended to express disrespect toward alternative medicine, its practitioners, or those who subscribe to it. I myself have enjoyed various types of holistic treatment over the years and will be more than happy to share evidence of the positive effects of these treatments with those interested, the moment means are found to detect such a thing.

19
A Better Pill to Swallow

Fun is not subject to measurement and quantification. In fact, it violates the basic principles of mathematics. This is readily demonstrated by the following simple equation: 3 x (fun-sized Mars Bar) = 1 regular Mars Bar. Where did the fun go?

Principia Chocolatica, 1687

A journey of a thousand miles begins with a single step toward the mall in order to buy the necessary supplies and equipment. The next steps are collecting information, planning travel routes, and sorting out legal papers and sleeping arrangements. The last step is finally setting out on the spontaneous journey. Bon voyage.

Laozi proverb

Since the dawn of industrial pharmaceutics, mankind has been faced with one of history's greatest mysteries: why don't they just make pills twice the size? *They* know it, *we* know it, *everyone* knows it—we're all adults and children above the age of twelve, and we're going to be taking two pills, so why mess about? Just make them twice as big and save us the effort. How many minutes upon minutes are wasted throughout the lifelong medicinal career of the average pill-taker, popping open all those extra cards, valuable time that could be better utilized for productive activity such as grumbling and complaining?

At least that's what I used to think. Then they hit me with the calcium pill. I'm not sure if that's its official name, but that's how it will remain etched into my memory, and throat, forever. This life-changing encounter took place during my stay at bone marrow inn, at a time when my diet consisted mainly of a variety of pills, antiseptic mouthwashes, and the faint memory of happiness. One would imagine that under such circumstances, the introduction of a new pill to my daily rattling shot glass would hardly be much of an inconvenience. If anything, it could almost be considered an exciting and exotic side dish of sorts.

But the calcium pill was different. The method employed by such a pill, it would appear, is to attempt to restore your bone structure by swallowing the complete skeleton of a fully grown, medium-sized mammal, conveniently compressed into a pill just slightly smaller than the complete skeleton of a fully grown, medium-sized mammal.

You're probably wondering what the big fuss is. Just break it in half. Break that pill in half right down that ever-so-slightly indented center line that somehow, by reducing the pill's thickness to only 99.9 percent of its original unsnappable bulk, will surely enable an easy and accurate break.

But real men don't break pills in half. Real men are far too busy bringing in the shopping in one massive go, bags dangling from every semi-available grip-worthy joint, progressing at a pace that guarantees the spoiling of all perishables, not because leaving the tenth bag behind is in any way a challenge to their male ego, but "because it's quicker this way." So how in the world are we expected to find the time to be splitting all sorts of pills in half and carrying out other such unnecessary laborious activities?

So, I snapped it in half. It was much better—I got to enjoy the experience twice, with the added bonus of sharp edges scraping my esophagus. The parts, somehow, were far greater than the sum of their whole.

When we were kids, we were spared the evil of pills, and a bit of syrup would do the trick. Contrary to the teaching of the child-minding guru Mary Poppins, we live in a time when, rather than needing a spoonful of sugar to help the medicine go down, a spoonful of medicine seems to contain, somehow, several spoonsful of sugar, in a variety of flavors. One can endure a perfectly tolerable sickness at no peril whatsoever. Years passed, and with time we reached the point at which the necessary dose of syrup would require a large beer mug, and so we graduated to pills. Crushed, of course, and mixed into a spoonful of jam. We matured, and tentatively took half a pill with a large glass of juice. Later we dared and took a whole pill, throwing our heads back triumphantly, confident that we could now surely face any dish life had to serve us. But as we aged, we learned that life has many pills to offer, and some are larger and more bitter than others. And sometimes, the only way to swallow them is one little bit at a time.

When I was discharged from my month-long stay in the hospital, I arrived home and started my recovery process. I wanted to do everything: walk, talk, read, write, eat, drink, and other such exciting activities of the kind that usually decorate our bucket lists. But I found that I couldn't do anything, which is infinitely less than everything. I also "wanted" to take all my pills, a daily handful of colorful little gems, but I couldn't. By that point, the abuse to my digestive system—the nausea, the vomiting, the bloating, and the cramps—had brought me to a point where the mere thought of a pill's chalky surface crawling down my throat was utterly repulsive and triggered a gag reflex. I started falling behind on my medication, which naturally posed a real threat to my health. When I shared this with my immunologist during a following checkup appointment, I got a proper telling-off. She gave me a look that made me feel like a misbehaved child.

And then it hit me. A child. That's exactly what I needed to be. I suddenly realized that I didn't have to take all my pills at once. I could split up my troubles into bite-sized nibbles. You'd be surprised how far baby steps can take you. Ask anyone who once was one. Most of them are nowhere near the delivery room by now, and some have gone quite far in life indeed.

20
Don't Be My Guest

Blood [noun]—a red liquid that circulates in the arteries and veins of humans and other vertebrate animals, and is thicker than water, though not as refreshing a cold beverage.

The Complete Dictionary of Incomplete Truths

There are many thoughts in a man's heart. Most of them don't involve your well-being.

Mishlei Emmett 19:21

Some people can't seem to tell the difference between being full of thoughts and being thoughtful. Personally, I think that people like that are rubbishful.

The various relationships we form with other people throughout our lives describe a complex set of intertwining geometric shapes on the graph paper of our hearts. Whether broad or narrow, well-defined or blurry-lined, even or asymmetric, isolated or overlapping, these patterns produce a map portraying the scope, structure, and nature of our human interactions.

Our picture usually starts with a single point, the size and position of which on the map are probably a function of one's self-esteem. The ultimate focal point. The surrounding shape is typically elliptical, drawn around the two foci that are one's self and one's significant other. To be precise, this is probably better described as two partially overlapping circles. Or at least that's what I was led to believe in an early twenties pre-dating group counseling session (by "early twenties" I mean the age group, not the decade. In the years 1920 to 1925, I was not yet ready for a serious relationship, and by 2020 I was already deeply invested in one). The instructor split us into pairs and handed out small slips of paper and pencils, and two lengths of rope per pair. We were then told to draw two circles and tie the ropes together in a knot in a way that best represents marriage. I'm not entirely sure what the "correct" answer was, or if perhaps the purpose of the exercise was to show that there is in fact no one right answer that fits all. I think I stopped listening when the speaker's opening "hello" clashed with my full concentration on the refreshments. Not wanting to totally exclude ourselves from the group activity, my teammate and I drew the two circles as a pair of handcuffs and tied the ropes into a noose. I still think that our representation was more accurate than most others. The instructor begged to differ. I think that in terms of art, we were simply divided between realism and idealism. Somewhat ironically, my accomplice and I were the first two of the group to find our respective better halves and tie the knot. I very much hope that in this case life won't imitate art.

Stretching beyond the spousal representation are rings of neighboring immediate family members, each two relationships creating a triangle, a three-way relationship comprising three two-way relationships. Wider and wider circles of extended family, friends, work colleagues, and acquaintances follow, until the outlines slowly fade into the general blur of mankind.

Of these relationships, few, if any, possess the qualities that make the sharing of certain experiences bearable, if not completely comfortable. A good example of such an experience would be spending an afternoon together in a small hospital room, conversation limited mainly to a series of groans and grunts, entertainment primarily a sequence of stomach cramps and nausea and, generally speaking, long stretches of silence.

There really aren't many people in one's life that can join one for such an afternoon and be a comforting presence rather than an uncomfortable invasion, which is why I limited my company to the narrow inner circle of immediate family. But it turned out that other people wanted a piece of the action, too. This is where thoughtful and thoughts-ful crossed paths or, to be accurate, collided.

Throughout my hospital stay I had taken to the habit of not answering my phone, an impolite privilege I felt myself entitled to at the time, and I relied on my wife to screen my calls. This habit proved quite hard to break for some time later and resulted in the D section of my contacts becoming somewhat crowded with a group of people who shared the name "Don't Answer," proving, perhaps, that some personality traits are indeed genetically determined.

One such screen-worthy call came from a certain individual, kindly offering to pay a visit. The offer soon gave way to a request, and finally graduated into a claim to rights. Visiting a cancer patient, I was informed, is not just about the patient and his best interests. Visitors have needs, too. They have a need to offer support, alleviate suffering, and to generally just be there for themselves—I mean, for you. And it is inconsiderate, indeed downright selfish, to deny them those needs. How dare I?

Those cancer patients, what are they like—always thinking about themselves. Absolutely thoughtless.

21
Goodbye, Sweetie

Life is like a box of chocolates—mostly empty.

Openwood Dulwitt

The opposite of chocolate is not vanilla. It's misery.

Scoop of the Day

Life is a stream of moments. A flow of fractional and all but nonexistent instants, never standing alone; flickers of future surging into the past, brushing lightly against an illusory present in their flight. But some moments stand out, when the river of time seems to freeze over and allows us to rest gently on its surface, spared the perpetual motion of its current. So pivotal are such moments that they define time itself, finely splitting one's life—indeed the history of mankind—into "before" and "after"; "pre-" and "post-"; "what preceded" and "that which is to follow." Basically, in two.

For me, one such moment involved a bar of chocolate and a can of Coke, and things have never been the same since.

The time is summer, the place is the hospital, and the mood is a bit of both. It's two weeks after my transplantation, and I'm in my private room (i.e., isolation), sitting on a chair beside my bed. The small room I occupy, all day, every day, boasts four sitting options, not including the floor and the toilet: a bed, an armchair (a generous description) to one side of the bed, a low one-seater sofa (a description that goes beyond generosity and into the realm of wastefulness) that unfolds into an uneven mattress, and a chair (a fair description). For the better part of the day, every day, all four of these sitting apparatuses are occupied, by me. Not simultaneously, but close enough to confuse any innocent passerby. They say that variety is the spice of life, but sometimes you have no life and no spice, and all you have is variety, in its most bare and minimal form—a change of perspective. Not a profound change in outlook, or a new view of the world; a literal change of perspective—a new view of the room, from an ever-so-slightly different angle. A time-lapse video of my average day at the time would be quite a sight, featuring as its sole content a blurry image spinning around the room about the fixed axis of an IV pole, impossibly occupying all spaces at all times, very much an unending and erratic version of human string-ball.

When there's nothing to do, you do nothing, but you try to do it in a hundred different ways.

I'm sitting on chair number one, and my wife arrives. (I never figured out exactly what the terms of my "isolation" were, as visitors, within limits, were allowed. There was a double set of doors, the windows were sealed shut, and a ventilation system constantly ran, drawing out the "used" air and all traces of happiness.) She asks me, as she does every day, if she can get me anything to eat or drink.

A word about my diet: For the better part of a four-week hospital stay, my daily intake consisted of three liters of saline and the smaller half of a slice of toast. It wasn't so much that I couldn't eat, rather that I didn't want to. The whole concept of a physical desire to consume food was foreign, nothing but an abstract and distant intellectual notion. Slowly, as the days went by, vague memories of food and the lost pleasures it once held started surfacing, bearing promising signs of what might one day lead to a faint shadow of an appetite.

"Yes," I respond, in a moment of euphoria, from chair number two. "Maybe I *will* have something to eat. And drink. Not just *some*thing; *the* things. The ultimate things of things: a bar of chocolate and a can of Coke. Chocolate and a Coke are what I want—in fact what I *need*! I shall not survive one more moment unless a bar of chocolate and a can of Coke are brought to me with great immediacy!" I fumble clumsily for the nurse-summoning clicker—just out of reach from my position in chair number three—in a desperate and senseless attempt to speed up the process, to make known the extent of this sudden emergency.

Chocolate and Coke. Those two crowns of culinary excellence. True feats of human ingenuity. A celebration of cerebral superiority. Two of the greatest achievements of mankind. Basically, good stuff.

Sitting on the bed, my eyes follow my wife's hurried footsteps as she departs on her holy mission, her palate-pleasing pilgrimage. I count the minutes longingly, eagerly waiting to celebrate the return of my meager appetite, the regeneration of gastronomical gratification. Time crawls by, and finally, after an agonizing five minutes that feel at least like six, she appears, treasures in hand. She places them before me.

I pause, savoring the moment. I caress the can lovingly, running my hand over its smooth, cold surface. Slowly, I slide my fingernail under the edge of the tab, raising it slightly, and then abruptly yank it open. And there it is. That most coveted of all audio-sensory pleasures. That angelic two-note musical masterpiece, composed by chemistry, perfected by physics: "*Crack-tshhh.*" Ahh. And now for the kill. I raise the can to my mouth, pressing it to my lips and draw the customary long first pull, the one after which the rest is really just unwanted leftovers. In an instant, my whole being is overcome by the sharp, cool, sweet, bitter, vanilla-hinting, caramelly flavor hitting thousands of craving taste buds.

It's disgusting.

The chocolate soon follows, this time without ceremonial prelude. I can't believe my tongue. It's official—my taste buds are fried. Until that moment, I was aware of five major taste groups: sweet, sour, salty, bitter, and umami (whatever that one actually means). But it turns out that there's a sixth taste: cancer. And, surprisingly, it turns out that it's actually quite a common flavor. Indeed, from that moment on, everything I ate tasted of it. So vile was this new-coming and evil vanquisher that in a blitzing craze, it conquered my entire world of flavors, taking all others captive and rendering them nothing more than nuanced slaves to its overpowering dominance. Basically, everything was yucky.

"It's quite normal," I was told upon inquiry (a curious use of the word "normal," but after one is exposed to such creative use of words for a while, the phenomenon becomes quite normal). "This type of chemotherapy affects the digestive system, taste buds included. In fact, you should consider yourself quite lucky; many of the patients in the ward can't eat at all—they have to be fed intravenously." Actually, I always wondered what it would be like to take cola intravenously. This might be my chance.

It took a few weeks until some sort of taste normality returned, and a few months before eating could be experienced in a way that somewhat resembled pleasure. Even today, years later, my kids still regard with suspicion any food feedback I offer, and long gone are the days of my soup-tasting/flavoring authority.

But it's alright; with time I've come to learn that the way things really are and the way we perceive them are not always perfectly aligned. Oftentimes something that's sweet in essence can be experienced as sour, and that's OK; we still know it's good for us and go along with it even if it's not all that pleasant. And sometimes something might be very sweet and not all that good for us, and perhaps there's a blessing in not being fooled by sugarcoated delights. And maybe, armed with a new sense of sense, we can get better at swallowing some of the bitter pills life occasionally prescribes us.

22
Mask of Misery, Pillar of Pain

There are two types of people in the world: those who get on with things and live life to the fullest, and those who spend life pointlessly classifying people into two types.

Reflections on Reflections, 1881

Fine is the line that runs between living an entirely tolerable life and absolute misery. The small things in life truly defy the laws of gravity with the great weight they seem to carry and the crushing force they impose on us. If anyone tells you that the magnitude of suffering is inversely proportional to the square of the distance between you and a perfect life, you should probably start seriously questioning the sort of people you hang out with.

When weighing the pros and cons of beard-bearing, one of life's hairier decisions, one naturally considers the more obvious aspects of this facial feature: appearance and maintenance. You hardly consider the fact that when you'll have your impacted wisdom teeth surgically removed, your beard, with its natural insulative property, will prolong the pain by rendering ice packs ineffective. And you certainly don't anticipate the additional inconvenience your beard will lend to the paper mask wearing that your future cancer will necessitate.

Soon after my bone marrow transplantation and before my beard and I went on trial separation, when my white blood cells went on strike, I was faced with a moment-by-moment choice between two forms of torment: I could either stay cooped up in my small room, mask free, or I could roam free through the ward corridors, in masqueraded misery.

It's hard to properly describe the quality and extent of discomfort caused by wearing a paper mask,[1] particularly for individuals such as myself, who sport glasses, a beard, and sensory issues: the elastic digging into the soft skin behind the ears; the flexible wire running along the top of the mask rubbing against the sensitive skin of the nose; the stiff upper edge interfering with the glasses, while your breath steams up the lenses; the stuffy, hot, paper-smelling air trapped in the mask; and the beard…the beard. I wasn't even particularly heavily bewhiskered, but it was enough to make the otherwise unpleasant experience unbearable.

Looking back, I'm not quite sure why I didn't just shave. It seems all too simple in hindsight. Perhaps I was desperately trying to maintain some sort of recognizability, to cling on to the familiar image of my former self. In a way, my beard was a strange form of extremely uncomfortable comfort.

And so it came to pass that I spent the month of my hospital stay almost exclusively in my tiny room, where, if nothing else, I didn't have to lose face.

Not that I had much energy for long leisurely strolls, but being trapped in a room for weeks makes the prospect of a walk down a hospital hallway seem like an exotic holiday. And the IV pole does double up as rolling walker of sorts. Or at least it would, if its wheels weren't made using the same ingenious mechanical system that is employed in supermarkets around the globe to make sure that shopping trollies glide smoothly in every possible direction except the one you want to go in.

IV poles are another example of what would seem to be—in the big cancer scheme of things—a minor irritation, but in fact turn out to be a central axis of anguish. An outsider, watching a patient trudge

---

[1] These lines, written before the COVID era in which face masks became a universal lifesaving inconvenience, seem pathetically whiny. But, for some reason, the world's future suffering didn't retroactively alleviate mine at the time. Thanks for nothing.

by clutching on to the clanking pole beside him, may think to himself, "That must be a bit annoying, having to drag that thing around." And perhaps, under the "normal" circumstances of a short treatment, it isn't much more than that. But when you're admitted for a transplantation and a PICC line is inserted, due to fear of blockage and infection you are hooked up to the pole for the entire duration of your stay, with not one moment of freedom of movement.

This unusual reality has a few unexpected effects. First and foremost, it means that in general, you start to consider and reconsider just how much you really need to do the things you want to do that involve moving. At first, the additional effort of taking the pole with you wherever you go, which is a bit like taking a mutated and very reluctant pet for a walk, is negligible. But it soon becomes burdensome enough to make you think twice before going to the toilet. Then you reach the point in which, even within the room, the thought of dragging the pole becomes a significant factor, so you position it in a central focal point in the room and from that moment on restrict your movement to the area of your new and constricted circle of life.

Changing and showering pose an interesting challenge, too. Needless to say, the pole has to accompany you to the shower, a violation of privacy of sorts already. But the real problem is that, due to the laws of physics, your clothes tend to follow you, too. This calls for a true feat of contortionism, in which the saline bag needs to be unhooked from the pole, threaded through the sleeve of your semi-removed shirt, and then placed back on the hook. Until fully mastered, this undertaking can result in the bag, your clothes, and you yourself being hooked onto the pole in various states of entanglement.

And then, to end the day, you have the "IV Pole Sleeping Dilemma." In this tricky trial, you have to decide on which side of the bed to position the pole before you futilely attempt sleep, in order to minimize discomfort. In truth, a coin flip would be equally as effective as the greatest minds put to work on this cunning conundrum, since in your sleep you will toss and turn in both directions and, at some point, inevitably find yourself wrapped in the IV cord and your own arm.

And so it was, that to avoid inconvenience and discomfort I hardly left my hospital room and paid the high price of restriction. My room was safe. My room was easy.

Don't we all live that way, afraid to go out without our masks, afraid to go out and do what we know is best, just because it's inconvenient or hard? Perhaps it wouldn't be such a bad thing if we cast away our costumes and pulled away from our pillars, just every now and then. Who knows how far we could go?

23
Hair Today, Gone Tomorrow

Hi, we're "Don't give me that look" and "Look at me when I'm talking to you," and these are our kids, "What are you looking at?" "How do I look?" and "Mommy, Daddy, look at me!"

What to Expect When Meeting Your Expectations, p. 1

Don't look at the container but at that which is in it. But if, when you look in it, it turns out to be empty, take a look at the container; it might be worth something at the marketplace.

Ethics of the Farmers 4:21

The kids were disappointed. Every morning it was the same story. No matter what medium of communication we used—phone, Skype, FaceTime, WhatsApp video call—the result was always the same. I still had hair.

But Daddy…you promised that this time your hair will fall out!

It was bad enough that after six months of chemotherapy I still had a full head of hair. Now, a whole week had passed since the transplantation and still nothing, not a single hair on my head had the common decency to fall out.

Why, you may ask, were my kids so anxious and keen on the idea of me losing my hair? What was this bald notion that they simply couldn't seem to brush off? Well, it turned out to be a matter of great family honor.

"Aba...you don't understand, none of my friends believe that you have cancer." They don't? Well, that settles it then—I clearly don't. I must be cured! Who would have thought that a dash of disbelief was all it takes? This has to be the discovery of the century! I must rush and contact all cancer research institutes and share the wonderful news. "Guys, you'll never believe this...No! I didn't mean to say that! Don't not-believe it, then it won't work! Really—my kids' friends told me—anything you disbelieve doesn't exist! Aagghh! I can't believe it. Oops. I believe I've managed to confuse myself. Call you later."

And they weren't kidding (unless of course we define "kidding" literally as "acting in accordance with the manner in which kids do," in which case pretty much everything they do is kidding). One day, I was picking up my then-seven-year-old daughter from school, and, upon seeing me, her friend said, "You don't look like you have cancer." I asked her what cancer looked like. "I don't know," she replied, "but I don't think it smiles." "Actually," I said, "cancer wears whatever expression you pick out for it that day."

And so, it became a daily routine; at some point each day, I gave my hair a yank, not quite sure what to expect or hope for. On one such day, my mother called with news. Apparently, she had it on good Google authority that day twelve was when the magic happened. Of course, I disregarded this piece of information and took it as utter cyber-babble. After all, I was inclined to disbelieve all wiki cancer wisdom, not the least due to the fact that it had previously offered me a life expectancy of only three to five years, some sixty years less than I had originally scheduled myself. Ridiculous.

On day twelve my hair fell out.

Well, the first handful fell out, and by "fell" I mean "was tugged," in the first-ever successful attempt of my newly adopted custom. The rest followed shortly after, and by "followed" I mean that I scrubbed off as much of it as I could in a hair-washing frenzy. The experience culminated in the dramatic slow-motion head-raise toward the mirror. I stood by the sink, arms resting heavily on either side for support, tense with apprehension, prepared for the worst, hoping for the best, and quite sure of finding something in between. The reality was none of the above. When I looked up, I found that I had simply showered myself into old age, a thinned-out version of my previous self. The rest was then trimmed into extinction.

Still staring at the semi-familiar image reflected in the mirror, I found great comfort in the fact that my beard was still intact. A broad grin stretched slowly across my face. They say that smiling is a very powerful tool. Indeed, this smile was so strong that it left bald patches on my cheeks in its wake. So much for the full beard. Throughout the day, aided by much chin stroking and a trimmer, the patchwork of face-fuzz was reduced to a goatee, a mustache, a pencil mustache, and eventually a faint memory. Now the real magic happened. If losing my hair had aged me by ten years, losing my beard knocked off twenty (if we include the ten that were just added). It wasn't the look I had hoped for, but it was a reality that I would just have to face up to.

The next morning, my mother came to visit. I hadn't warned her about the sight she was about to encounter, but she didn't miss a beat and greeted me with the charming "Nice eyebrows!" I guess that when hair is present, eyebrows are just background scenery, but when the hair is gone eyebrows take center stage. I found comfort in my newfound eyebrows, and in being alive. I did a quick calculation and figured out that if my head was showing, it was a sure sign that I had a head, and for that, considering the alternative, one must surely be thankful.

To be perfectly honest, being bald was one of the most pleasant parts of my whole cancer experience. If you've never felt the refreshing sensation brought about by splashing cool water on your bare head first thing in the morning, well, then you've never felt it. I would use the worn-out phrase "words cannot describe," but I try to avoid that self-contradicting, nonsensical nugget. One can hardly expect to be taken seriously when using the words "words cannot describe"—which are most definitely words—to describe something, least of all something that cannot be described by words. But in all seriousness, pedantry aside, it's an amazing feeling, and I suddenly understood why so many people shave their heads. It turns out that it isn't actually just to save money on shampoo.

Speaking of shampoo and bald heads, as a newly-bald I was curious if I would still have use for my Head and Shoulders shampoo. Their website kindly informed me that dandruff does not occur on bald heads. Other skin irritations are available, but they aren't treatable by Head and Shoulders. I was quite impressed by their honesty and the fact that they hadn't simply marketed a whole line of products against "bald-head dandruff" or tried to get bald people to still buy their product to use on their shoulders. It seems that in regard to business ethics they are much better than many other companies. Indeed, it appears that they are (yes, you knew it was coming…) head and shoulders above the rest.

One last point on the subject of hairless washing: I can't not mention the time we had a plumber install a new shower drain filter, followed by a warning not to allow too much hair to clog the system, followed by a glance at my head, followed by awkward silence.

Having established myself as an official member of the bald community, much decision-making was ahead. The first step was to tackle the tricky matter of head-covering. The possibilities of what to place atop one's head are numerous, and it truly seemed as though the sky was the limit. I made my way through a list of options, off the top of my head, and their respective drawbacks:

- Nothing—will look too much like a cancer patient.
- Bandana—will look too much like a pirate.
- Wooly hat—will look too much like a cancer patient.
- Toupee—will look too much like a toupee.
- Baseball cap—will look too much like a cancer patient.
- All of the above— will look like an idiot. With cancer.

In the end, I went for the "natural" look, providing that we consider chemotherapy-induced hair-loss natural. I did it because I was proud of my bald head—the mark of my martyrdom, the symbol of my struggle. But mainly because the other options looked awful.

Losing my hair was one of the first things I thought of and worried about when I was first diagnosed, even though I was told it would only occur at a much later stage of my treatment regimen. In that, I'm sure

I'm not alone. It may seem trivial compared to the vast array of side effects and diminished quality of life that were expected, but I'm not sure that anxiety cares much for such rational arguments. What would I look like? Will I be embarrassed to go out in public? How will I keep my *kippah* on? But, as it turned out, and I can only speak for myself, from my own personal experience, temporary hair loss wasn't the turbulent, tangled episode I feared it would be. In fact, the whole experience came and went quite smoothly. Seriously, if we waste a good worry on every little trifle that pops up, we may not have enough worry left in us when we really need it for the worry-worthy whoppers of life. And that truly is a worrying thought.

24
Crash Course

People say that money makes the world go round. I beg to differ. Earth spins because it formed in the accretion disk of a cloud of hydrogen that collapsed down from mutual gravity and needed to conserve its angular momentum. It continues to spin because of inertia. And money.

A. Richman

A laptop crashing isn't the rarest of events. A laptop-crushing, on the other hand, is slightly less common. But I still managed one, and in style.

The ward I was hospitalized in was particularly sensitive and attentive to the needs of its patients and dedicated to providing them with maximum comfort. In order to offer them peace of mind and keep them informed of their ever-changing medical conditions, they made sure that the daily blood test results would be available each morning in time for the doctors' rounds.

The fact that this undertaking involved routinely waking us at 4:00 a.m. to take blood was, apparently, for our own good. Indeed, it was just what the doctor ordered.

My last such rendezvous, which took place in the early morning hours of what would later turn out to be the day of my long-awaited discharge, appeared to be unexceptional in every way: Nurse walks in. Light on. Sorry to wake you. It's alright, I wasn't asleep anyway—that tends to happen when you don't sleep. I'm just going to raise the bed with this button. Electric humming noise. Arm stretched out. Syringe slurp. OK, we're done here, enjoy lying wide awake waiting patiently for dawn so you can continue feeling sick in a variety of different positions. You can lower your bed now. Light off.

I'm not quite sure why they had to raise the bed in the first place. I don't remember any of the nurses being seven feet tall or any of the beds being two feet high. But raised it was, and now it was time to lower it. Button. Electric humming noise. Resistance. Strange, it's usually quite a smooth ride. Electric humming noise. Bed lowered.

In the morning there was a surprise waiting for me. Before retiring for the night, I had carefully placed my laptop in its case and propped it up against the side of the bed for safekeeping. During the bed-raising procedure that night it must have slipped ever so slightly and gotten caught, still in a vertical position, under the bed. Hence the difficulty lowering the bed, and a rare opportunity to answer the age-old question: electric bed vs. laptop—who will win? I opened the case to find not so much a laptop but a pile of technological rubble. So long, my old friend, and a considerable amount of not-backed-up material.

But there was no time for mourning. Discharge was afoot, packing was ahead, and homecoming was at hand.

The thought of being stuck at home for the two-month recovery period without a computer was quite worrisome, so we decided to buy a new one on our way home, in the mall adjacent to the hospital. As we were walking toward the shop, I commented to my wife jokingly that perhaps I would get a pity discount for being a cancer patient. Wouldn't it be great if the hospital records and the shops' computer systems were somehow linked to each other, and all prices were corrected to match the degree of *nebach*-ness of each customer? But since, as of now, my ingenious system does not exist, they'll be unaware of my condition, and I'm not entirely comfortable bringing it up. One hates to brag about these matters. She gave me the look she reserves for those not-so-rare occasions in which I say something so utterly ridiculous that it's hard to believe I've managed to go through life this far without my mini-species of one going extinct on account of intellectual inadaptability. "You're in a hospital mall. You look like the walking dead. There's not a hair on your head. You're wearing a mask, and your wife is carrying your bags. I think they might pick up on some of those subtle hints and figure out that you're not exactly in Olympic shape."

She was right, of course. But we still didn't get a discount. I asked the man behind the counter if he could help me by recommending the cheapest laptop in stock, and he fetched it for me from the storage room. "This model comes with a long list of technical terms that you don't understand but have to nod your head to lest you appear moronic, not tech-savvy, and susceptible to advantage-taking. It also comes with a one-year warranty. Will sir, um, be needing that?"

"I'll take the laptop, thanks. And a long life to you, too."

25
Sir Cancer Can

Talking to yourself is the first sign of a good conversation.
The voice in your head

There's a lot we can learn from cancer. Not from *people* with cancer. There's probably a lot we can learn from them, too, but we can learn a lot from *cancer*—cancer itself. After all, what is cancer? Cancer is, technically speaking, a life form that has one function—to propagate, multiply, and affect as many systems as possible. So devoted is this entity to achieving its goal that, to fully succeed, it must inevitably make the ultimate sacrifice: die for its cause. Left to its own devices, without being "hindered" by treatments, this unwanted guest will eventually kill its host, thereby killing itself. Such is the selfless nature of its existence.

Perhaps cancer has taken things a bit too far. Having no independent value, existing purely to affect others, is not a true ideal. Misplaced altruism is not a virtue; it's a perversion of one. But there is a lesson to be learned about dedication, persistence, and the tremendous impact we have on the circles we belong to, for better or worse, intended or accidental. We've been put here on this small planet all together for a reason, not for lack of space in a vast universe. We can, we do, and we must have an effect on our surroundings. And we should make it a significant one. If a bunch of damaged cells can do it, we certainly can.

26
Outpatients and Inmates

If crime doesn't pay, you're definitely robbing the wrong bank.

Nerves of Steal, p. 100

Risk, concern for well-being, and fear of death are hardly foreign concepts in an oncology ward. But sometimes the threat comes from an unexpected source.

During one visit to the outpatient clinic, I shared a room with a prisoner, who, in addition to being chained intravenously to various colored bags of liquid life like the rest of us, was also handcuffed and heavily guarded. The blood of a benevolent donor, given for a noble cause, flowing into the hand that perhaps spilled another's, for a cause no less noble in his eyes. I'm not sure what crime this young man committed, but the fact that he was guarded by three armed police officers implied quite strongly that it probably involved crossing a red line, not a red light.

On another occasion, we were sitting across from the lift (a platform or compartment housed in a shaft for raising and lowering people or things to different floors or levels), when suddenly the doors slid open and out filed four armed[1] private security guards. I was somewhat surprised, since there was no word of any celebrity scheduled to visit

---

1   Microsoft Word's insistent autocorrect suggestion "four-armed private security guards" describes a much more exciting image, but I decided to opt for authenticity.

the ward. When the protected one finally emerged, he turned out to be a frail, elderly, wheelchair-bound rabbi.

Three guards for a prisoner, four for an old sage. Apparently, religious leaders are in greater danger of "attack" by overzealous followers, or attack without quotation marks from their no less zealous objectors, than the general public is by convicted criminals.

Indeed, hospitals are no place for an ill person. Or a healthy one for that matter. You never know what dangers lurk there.

27
Know Thy Place

Location, location, location. Isn't everything, isn't everything, isn't everything, in life.

The Incomplete Guide to Unreal Estate, p. 111

Know where you came from and where you're going. But sometimes, do yourself a favor and pretend you don't know where you are.

I have been visiting the outpatient clinic for several years now. Throughout this time, the visits have varied much in frequency, but not in format. The experience is remarkably similar every time, creating a strange sense of familiarity, irrespective of the length of the intervals.

My wife and I usually choose to spend the day and receive my treatment in the general waiting area, on regular chairs, and not in the designated and "classic" treatment room—the one with the armchairs, as seen on TV. We forgo this comfort because the treatment room, or "God's waiting room," as some insensitive cynics call it (I, of course, would never refer to it so crudely in public), is a tad on the dismal side. Multiple myeloma is more popular among senior folk, with the average age at the time of diagnosis being "quite old." Only 2 percent belong to my group of under-forties. Naturally, I am therefore somewhat of a youngster in the ward and feel as though I don't quite belong in the gloom room. Besides, if we do sit there, I have to feign sleep when the exercise and meditation instructors come by to offer their free and allegedly freeing services and enlighten us about the importance of moving and not moving, respectively. We sit instead in the open area outside the ward, reading books and chatting, glancing occasionally at a barely audible wall-mounted television that boasts a repertoire of one channel, mostly showing cooking shows. "This delicious dish is easy to make, elegant, and guaranteed to impress your dinner guests. All you need is someone else to buy, wash, weigh, and prepare all the ingredients in small glass bowls and preheat the oven. And here's one the producers made earlier. Thank you all for watching. I've been Chefy McChef, and I bid you bon appétit. Enjoy feasting tonight on a lovely, steaming-hot microwave dinner for one."

Be it a semiweekly, weekly, or monthly visit, the coffee-making kerfuffle never fails to materialize. We settle down and my wife asks if I'd like a coffee. Not being much of a drinker, I thank her for her kind offer and, knowing that she's about to make one for herself, offer to do it for her. This sincere and seemingly innocuous gesture, however, is greeted with strong opposition. "There is no way in this world I'm letting you make me a hot drink," is her response. "Over my dead body," she adds courteously.

A bit of background might be necessary here. In every household, in order for the establishment to function in a satisfactory manner, different roles must be assumed by the various occupants of the house. One such task, for which I am quite famous house-wide, is the making of hot drinks. Personally, I pride myself on the unusual and outstanding lifelong achievement of never having drunk a cup of tea. This is due to a combination of an extremely nonviolent rebellion against conformity to social norms, and not liking tea. But tea- and coffee-maker of the house I am, spending seconds upon seconds every day selflessly boiling, brewing, pouring, stirring, and serving my wife tea and coffee on demand (and by that I don't mean "as soon as or whenever required." I mean *on demand*).

With this in mind, it's always somewhat of an oddity, though no longer a surprise, when on a hospital day she refuses to keep up our marital arrangement. "I just don't understand. I made you a drink right before we left for the hospital, and I'll be making you one when we arrive home, so why in the world can't I make you one now?"

"Because now it's different! Now we're in the hospital to receive your treatment. Now you're a cancer patient. Now you will sit and do nothing for yourself or anyone else, like the helpless, weak man that you aren't!"

And so, she makes her own drink, and all that remains for me is to muse over the extraordinarily powerful impact an environment has upon one. At times it seems that where we are, not only influences us, but defines us, at least in the eyes of others. But my real fear is that sometimes it convinces even *us* to be something other than ourselves. When in Rome, by all means, do as Romans do, whatever it is that Romans get up to these days.[1] But when in the hospital, do me a favor, be yourself. The place is gloomy enough as it is; it doesn't need misery-by-proxy sprinkled in for good measure. There's plenty of *HaMakom yenachem eschem* in the world; there's no need for *HaMakom yetza'er eschem*, too.

If you do find yourself in the hospital, and you happen to find me there, too, and you just so happen to be in the mood to heal the world and make it a better place, or just to heal me and make me a better drink, it's one flat teaspoon of coffee, two heaped sugars—one white, one brown—very hot water, and just enough milk to give it flavor and texture without cooling it down. If you really must make me your charitable act of the day, go ahead, but do it right. I'm allowed *some* standards. I may have lost my coffee-making privileges, but I shouldn't have to lose my coffee-enjoying rights, too.

---

[1] It would be remiss not to mention an unrelated incident related to this phrase. An Italian student from Milan once asked me the following *sh'eilah*. When visiting the Great Synagogue of Rome, should she daven according to her regular *nusach* or according to *nusach Roma*? Delighted at being served possibly the greatest joke setup of all time, I responded, "When in Rome, do as the Romans do." My delight was immediately surpassed by my disappointment when the lack of a reaction revealed that one thing Romans don't do is use this phrase.

28
Over the Hills and Far Away

Given the choice, I would choose to not have choices.

Choice Quotes, page of your choice

By this point in human history, or human psychology to be precise, we know very well that the grass isn't really always greener on the other side. It's usually our eyes, green with envy, that lend it that hue. But when it comes to our problems, serious ones in particular, we still tend to assume that the solutions are only to be found far from home. In nature, gravity draws things closer to each other. But in life, it often seems that the gravity of any given issue has the opposite effect, as it places an ever-increasing distance between us and the solution. In other words, the universal law of "problem gravity" dictates that if we are "here," the answers must be "there," regardless of where we are.

The first stage of my treatment was quite straightforward, a generally accepted first line of offensive defense in the form of a medicinal cocktail, consisting of biological and chemical drugs, garnished with steroids, over a period of several months. The second stage, a bone marrow transplantation, was also standard procedure. But after the less-than-perfect results of those two first steps, I found myself in the twilight of medical uncertainty, immobilized by the weight of decision-making. I was at a four-way crossing, and these were the routes I could take:

1. Do nothing (incidentally, the name of my future autobiography, subtitled, "The one habit of highly ineffective people," sub-subtitled, "The story of my life," sole content: "Unfortunately

I haven't actually gotten around to writing this book yet. The end"). This option involved doing nothing.
2. Do very little (incidentally, my high school nickname. Teachers can be so cruel). This option involved a "maintenance" treatment plan. On paper, this was a safe and attractive option, with relatively little cost and some plausible benefit, but the inevitable run-down-vehicle connotation that the word "maintenance" conjured up drove me off that track.
3. Do quite a bit, which might turn out to be a lot, but also might turn out to be a lot of nothing (incidentally, not a particularly catchy name for anything). This third possibility involved taking part in a clinical trial testing out an experimental drug. Highly recommended by plenty of people who were not subject to the treatment, this course of action indeed sounded promising, providing that one kept in mind that one of the main characteristics of promises is that they are extremely fragile and easily broken. No one denies the tremendous importance of medical research and the critical role it plays in making advances in lifesaving and life-improving treatments. As long as the experiments are conducted on someone else. Guinea pigs, perfectly intolerable house pets as they may be, are hardly the subject of one's life aspirations. Even more off-putting was the knowledge that the trial involved a control group: a randomly assigned, unknowing two-thirds of the participants would be receiving placebos. This meant that taking part would present me with a 66.6 percent chance of investing a substantial amount of time and effort just to see if I could cure myself of cancer by the power of false belief. With all due respect to future cancer patients—my future-self included—the thought of finding out, after a year's investment, that my "medication" was a sugar pill, well, let's just say that that would be a bitter pill to swallow.
4. Do a considerable amount, for a possible considerable benefit, at a considerable cost (incidentally, no comment). The fourth and final option was to repeat three cycles of my original treatment

plan, aka chemo and bio à la steroids. This option held the extremely attractive prospect of possibly extending my remission by several years for the extremely unattractive price of enduring unpleasant side effects and the possibility of achieving nothing else but. This is where things became tricky, as they do with any risky investment. I decided to consult a fellow patient who had opted for this route, and apparently also opted to answer every question with an hour-long speech. The conclusion of his dissertation, put in my words, is that although in life there is no gain without pain, there is no shortage of pain without gain. And though rationally I knew that a survey of one hardly produces much of a statistic, the impression was hard to shake off. I fell victim to anecdotal bias. And if you, dear readers, are in any way swayed by my story, so have you.

Unable to make a decision I was fully comfortable with, I bode myself some time by way of contracting bronchitis-turned-pneumonia. Upon recovery, I was back at my four-way junction, and the lights were soon turning green.

Looking back now, I'm not quite sure why at the time this dilemma appeared to merit such extremely high levels of stress. But until the long-anticipated invention of a retrospectoscope, such time-bound anxieties will always be part of our lives.

Driven by doubt, I politely informed my doctor that I wished to pursue a course of investigation of my own, and embarked on an advice-seeking journey, confident that somewhere out there *the* answer was waiting to be found. I contacted specialists in various areas of medicine in various areas of the world and, after following a trail of names and numbers, reached what was alleged to be the ultimate database of medical advice: a particular individual regarded by many as the guru of remedial reference, the medical matchmaker. Naturally, contact with this contact master was not easily made. Unless special allowances were made, one would have to endure the long and steep climb up Mount Waiting List, something that could take quite some time. Fortunately, I found out that I knew someone who somehow knew something about someone who knew this medical monarch and was able to gain access to the coveted secret phone number. Of his assistant. After preparing all the relevant information for a comprehensive briefing and rehearsing my presentation, with much trepidation I placed the call. It lasted ten seconds. I started explaining my situation and he immediately cut me off and gave me the name of a doctor, *the* doctor, to consult. The name had a familiar ring to it, probably because it was the name of my doctor.

So I went back to square one and consulted my doctor. He recommended the clinical trial. I declined. He recommended the three-month treatment plan. I accepted. We all lived happily ever after. So far.

Sometimes we spend a lot of time and effort searching for something, certain that it must be somewhere out of reach, where all great things are, only to find that it was right under our noses all along. Appropriately so, perhaps, considering that one of the only places we can never really see is the area directly beneath our noses. It turns out that often we do indeed need other people's help, but not so much to solve our problems for us, rather to point out that we ourselves actually already have everything we need at our disposal. Once we only learn to appreciate that, we can stop looking "there" and start finding all the good things that are "here."

And in general, we really need to get better at trusting ourselves. Trust me, even if I myself don't.

29
What Makes You Tick?

Patience is the name of the game. You can cheat, but you're only cheating yourself, and when you "win," don't expect anyone to celebrate with you.

Jack and Malka Kenig

Time [noun]—a priceless commodity that you probably shouldn't waste on reading fake dictionaries.

The Complete Dictionary of Incomplete Truths

Drip.
Drip.

Drip.

Drip.

Actually, that's too generous a description. That would almost be tolerable. A depiction more befitting and closer to the truth would be Drip (long pause). Drip (agonizing time-stretch). Drip (sense-numbing slow-mo moment). Drip (this is going to take forever).

And then, after much anticipation and the painstaking pushing of the limits of patience, finally, the moment arrives. Drip.

They're very good at briefing you, the hospital people. They provide you with all manner of pamphlet and private consultation in order to best prepare you—physically, mentally, and emotionally—for the various experiences that will join forces and constitute the long and obstacle-filled journey of your treatment plan. "These are the drugs that will be administered to you"; "This will be the frequency of your visits"; "These are the side effects you should expect"; "These are some worrying symptoms that would require immediate attention"; "These are the names of twenty other booklets you should read just in case you're not yet sufficiently confused by the torrent of foreign terms and technical information."

But none of that helps. Not really. Does it really help to know that one of the three drugs you'll be given is called "dexamethasone"? Not really. What would really help would be if someone told you that when you drink it your taste buds will experience a vile encounter of unprecedented magnitude. In a weak attempt to communicate this indescribable "flavor," I would say that it was something akin to what I imagine it would be like if unsweetened cocoa, the tears of all mankind's pain and oppression, the Devil's gym socks, and the incessant righteous ramblings of a devout vegan met in a blender and then joined forces with the fermented carcass of an anthrax-plagued goat to create the world's most bitter and ghastly smoothie. I kid you not, the first time I took this drug and a cup of water did nothing to remove the vile, bitter taste from my mouth, I took a bite of my wife's leather purse in a sincere attempt to improve the situation. It would also be really helpful if someone told you that chasing it down with a sweet, milky coffee solves the problem. But that's apparently not important. That sort of intelligence pales in the face of the imminent and unequivocal need to be familiar with the proper technical term for the particular drug in question. Indeed, know thy enemy, at least by name.

They don't prepare you for the itchy nose. "In this episode of 'Wow, medical technology has really gone a long way since the days of drilling a hole in your skull to alleviate headaches,' we'll be draining all the blood from your body, running it through an apheresis machine, harvesting your stem cells, and reintroducing your blood into your body. No, you won't have to die and come back to life in the process." You'll be doing what?! OK, reap with joy, I guess. Just when you think you've mastered the art of aloofly taking IVs as a matter of routine, you find yourself sitting alongside an ominous, rumbling, vampire-like machine with a thick tube plugged into each arm. "This will take five hours, and if things go well, you'll only have to do it once." Only once? Sweet.

Sitting in an armchair for five hours doesn't sound like one of life's biggest challenges; indeed, many of us undertake such a task voluntarily on a daily basis. But there's a catch. This particular machine, with all its biochemical genius of separating blood into its various elements, has one critical weakness: it has a total breakdown if you bend your arms one nanometer. In such an (inevitable) event, much beeping and panic ensues, and the perfect position must immediately be reassumed. Seriously, they can land a probe on an asteroid, but they can't circulate a man's blood through a machine, harvest his stem cells, safely reintroduce the blood into his body, and save his life with his arms slightly bent! What a world.

Now, I'm not going to say that the average person doesn't fully appreciate his arms. Arms are clearly quite handy, and it's good to have them by our sides. I do think, though, that we're not quite aware of just how challenging it is to be so completely restricted, even for a relatively short period of time, while at full rest. Resisting the compulsion to bend your arms at the elbows is hard work. The soreness that kicks in is highly uncomfortable. It would help if they told you to do some arm warm-up exercises and stretches. It would help if they told you to bring comfortable, supportive pillows. And what would really help is if they told you that a patient would be well advised to make sure they are accompanied by a responsible adult, officially certified and available at all times for the purpose of nose scratching. You may, very possibly, have never experienced an itchy nose at any point in your life until now, but the moment your arms are trapped, your brain rebels in the most powerful way it can come up with—the uncontrollable torment of itching. Somehow, knowledge of the intricate workings of blood chemistry just doesn't seem to help overcome this affliction.

They don't prepare you for the dripping. At home, one of the walls of my bedroom sports a clock. I don't mean to brag. It's a simple timepiece, with a classic, timeless design. There is something somewhat special about it, though: it doesn't tick. This is not the rarest phenomenon when it comes to broken clocks, but this particular clock is actually in full working condition, obediently keeping time, its "second"/third hand seamlessly and soundlessly gliding about an expressionless, number-speckled face. This feat of engineering ingenuity—a smooth-sweeping second hand, a revolutionary improvement on hundreds of years of clockwork, has been a long time in the making. The difference between this type of clock and its traditional counterpart is literally night and day; one of them I can use by night, the other only by day.

   I'm a very light sleeper. To be accurate, I'm a very dark sleeper. I can't sleep with a light on, or with any other form of sensory input. You name it—light, noise, change in temperature, earthquake, anything at all—even if you name it very quietly, it will wake me. So a ticking clock is out of the question, and the smooth sweeper is a real lifesaver, or sleep-saver at least. But recently I've started losing sleep over this slick-circling time-teller. One evening, while sitting up in bed reading, my eyes were hypnotically drawn to its framed face, transfixed upon the unbroken motion of its second hand. An alarming thought seeped into my mind. Silently, with its unpausing persistence, my clock delivered a clear and sobering truth: there is no time. Not just no time *for* this and that and the other, but there literally *is* no time—no such thing as time, not in the present and tangible sense that we fool ourselves into believing in. At least a ticking clock, with its ever-stopping-and-going second hand, gives one the comforting illusion that the present moment does actually exist; that particular one moment in time toward which the hand is motionlessly pointing at this very moment, is now—is the here and now—and is courteously waiting for you for exactly one second before making way for its successor, who, in turn, will extend the same courtesy. This absolutely arbitrary unit of measurement—a sixtieth of a sixtieth of a twenty-fourth of the approximated duration of earth's average rotation—is time itself. But it isn't, of course. For any number of reasons, chief among them being that the dial on *my* clock doesn't pause on the second mark; its harsh hand glides coldly across the ever-aging face of time. But even my clock shows some kindness; it, too, is misleading. It doesn't tell the true time. Imagine an hourglass, with the finest of fine sands. Now imagine shattering the lower bulb and watching in horror as your sand/time/life steadily and irretrievably trickles away. That's an honest clock. True, it doesn't tell time, but it doesn't tell lies either. There *is* no time.

And still, whatever little illusory time we do have at our disposal, what do we do with it? All too often, just that—we dispose of it. Always waiting for the next thing, which, of course, will be so much better than its equally anticipated predecessor. We wait for the weather to improve and warm up, only to then wait for it to improve again and cool down; we wait for the weekend to free us from the tyranny of labor, only to then wait for the week to find respite from the demands of family life; we wait for night to give us rest from a long day, only to then lie in bed and wait for day.

Nothing can prepare you for the waiting. Nothing can prepare you for the tireless drip-drop and the endless tick-tock. Somehow, the ability to properly identify the excruciatingly slow-dripping toxin as "cyclophosphamide" just doesn't seem to help with that. You can go mad, sitting for hours doing nothing but counting drop after drop of clear liquid falling into a tube, waiting to be discharged. At some point you start convincing yourself, and your caring accompanier, that you've amassed enough medical knowledge, just by virtue of spending time in hospitals, to be your own judge of exactly how fast the IV *should* be dripping. "That looks very slow, don't you think? Is it usually that slow? It will be hours and hours at this rate. How much is left in there? It looks like a quarter, or half, or three-quarters, it's impossible to tell. This is going to take forever! I'll just loosen the valve a bit, speed things up, within the limits of what's certainly still safe, of course." On one such occasion, I must have overdone it, and perhaps also upset the nurse by trespassing on her professional property, because when she passed by and saw the fluid Niagara-Falling into my arm, she commented, "So, I take it you don't have any long-term plans for your kidneys?" and set the dripping back to a moderate snail pace. Indeed, many a foolish act has been committed upon desperation, and the mind-dulling experience commonly known as "waiting" is a desperation-inducing one like no other.

We find ourselves, time and again, stuck in situations that appear to have no intrinsic value, merely means to greater ends. But not all good means come to an end; some seem to go on and on forever, or in repetitive cycles. And these are substantial portions of our lives that we are carving out, throwing out, and missing out on. They say that life is 10 percent fact and 90 percent what you make of it. That's not true. Life is 10 percent fact, 90 percent waiting, and 100 percent what you make of those situations. And a multitude of other ingredients that make the formula extremely complex, much more accurate, and far less quotable.

The only thing we really control in life is how we react to each and every life situation. In that vein, there are many things we need to change our attitude toward, and we should certainly add waiting to the list.[1]

---

1   My repeated use of the phrase "they don't prepare you for" in this chapter and similar tones of writing are not intended as criticism of the hospital staff, and no, this isn't a setup for a joke about how it actually is. I have tremendous appreciation and gratitude to the multitude of healthcare professionals who were involved in my treatment. If your experience has been different, I strongly recommend that you urgently change either your treatment center or your personality.

30
Side-Burns

That which does not kill me has any number of potential effects on me, varying in nature and intensity, forming a seamless continuum of human experiences ranging from being a little bit irritating to making my life quite unpleasant indeed—pretty much any possible outcome other than death.

How to Philosophize with Tweezers 1:8

It's a strange thing, cancer. The illness kills but doesn't hurt; the treatment hurts but doesn't cure. Well, obviously the illness can hurt—does hurt, at some point, if left to do enough damage. But my point is that often, and certainly in my case, the pain and discomfort caused by the illness itself, at least in its initial stages, was minimal if at all present, whereas the treatment was a whole different story. I would go as far as putting forward a motion to reconsider the expression "battling cancer" and replace it with the more appropriate "battling cancer treatment." I worry, though, that my words will be taken out of context, and I'll be accused of promoting refusing treatment. That's unacceptable, and I refuse to be treated that way.

These challenging, often debilitating treatment-based inflictions of pain and misery are marketed under the deceptively subtle-sounding name "side effects," and they come in many shapes and forms.

The "classic" signature side effect of cancer treatment is, of course, nausea. Images of people with their heads down toilets—before, during, and after meals—decorate our television cancer references. Nausea comes in several variations: nausea without vomiting, nausea with vomiting, vomiting without nausea. What's the deal with nausea anyway? What is it? It's not really a form of pain. It's a whole new category of bad. On a scale of absolute bliss to Dante's Inferno, nausea is somewhere between extreme discomfort and bubonic plague. And there seems to be very little we can do to treat it. Upon admission to the bone marrow transplantation unit, the head nurse ran through the process with me and told me what joys I had to look forward to. Touching on the issue of nausea, he explained that although in regard to pain relief, modern medicine has gone a long way since the days of a swig of liquor, a bullet to bite on, and a good whack across the head, it hasn't made quite the same advances in treating nausea. For pain, a doctor can prescribe an array of pills, syrups, injections, and patches, individually or in a joint treatment. For nausea, on the other hand, the main thing a doctor can offer is condolences. Basically, he explained, as my later experience would confirm, there are three main drugs available, and, depending on the patient, they vary in degrees of how ineffective they are. This news was very worrying; in fact, it made me sick to my stomach.

A side effect less known to the "outside world," but perhaps even more challenging, is sleep deprivation. To a non-cancer-patient playing a word association game, the word "cancer" would surely be followed by the word "chemotherapy." But for many cancer patients, playing the actual game, the key word is "steroids." To a non-cancer-patient, still playing a word association game, the word "steroids" would surely be followed by the words "athlete," "bodybuilder," "muscles," and "questionable gold medals." For a cancer patient, by this point very fed up with the real-life game, steroids mean moody highs and lows, a fat face, and insomnia.

When I first started taking steroids, I was told that it might take me longer than usual to fall asleep. They were certainly right. It's been four years and I'm still waiting. Steroid-induced sleeplessness is its own type of insomnia. It's the impossible combination of being dead tired and wide awake, all the time. A bit like that numb-buzzing feeling that spreads through you when you are way past the point where coffee can help but you drink three espressos anyway.

The problem with being up all night, every night, besides the fact that after a couple of days your body and brain start crumbling into dysfunctional fragments, is that there's just not much to do. No matter how bad a situation is, throwing in a pinch of boredom is guaranteed to make it worse. You find yourself wondering at some point—I've already done some watching, I've already done some reading, I've already replied to some emails, I've already paced the house restlessly, I've already sat up in bed drinking soup from a mug, and I'm just about ready to go mad. And it's only 11:30!

My doctor was hesitant to prescribe sleeping pills. He said that I would become addicted to them and wouldn't be able to sleep without them. I told him that I already can't sleep without them, so I really have nothing to lose. "What about that dream you always had of operating heavy machinery?" he asked. "Don't worry about that," I responded. "That's just a line I wrote for you for comic effect."

I started with half a pill. When that stopped working, I moved on to a whole pill. Then I moved on to two pills. Then I moved on to a realization that it wasn't going well. I tried alternative sleep medication, and then I tried alternating between alternative and traditional sleep medication, and then I tried to remember why exactly I hadn't listened to my doctor in the first place.

I knew it wouldn't take long before the "have you tried bedtime breathing exercises" advice rolled in. But nevertheless, I waited. Being uncertified in matters of both breathing and exercise, I didn't want to take things into my own hands and self-medicate without expert counsel. I was told, on good authority, that the matter was of a complex scientific nature, and a professional and systematic approach was necessary. Therefore, in order to get the best results, I was to follow a very specific and tested procedure:

1. Go to YouTube.
2. Search, using the words "sleep," "breathing," "calm," "meditation," "relaxing," and "preferably not one with a particularly annoying voice."

3. Ignore all the videos that include the words "best," "most amazing," and "ten-hour version."
4. Pick one at random. They're all the same, anyway.

Sinister cynicism aside, I was actually in for a surprise. Well, to be honest, it was more of a shock than a surprise. I had asked my wife to join me for the experiment in case things got out of hand. After all the necessary preparations, i.e., lying down, I hit the play button. At first, not much happened. A side glance at my wife, a professional faller-asleeper, revealed that she had already fallen asleep. Then the video started playing. It started with some classic "find a comfortable position," "close your eyes," "relax," "tighten all your muscles," "relax all your muscles," "tighten these specific muscles," "relax those specific muscles," "feel the tension leaving this, that, and the other part of your body," and "somehow concentrate on all these anatomically detailed instructions while still maintaining maximum relaxation and no mental exertion." Then followed the much-anticipated "you're lying on your back in a field/beach/meadow/desert island/inflatable lake-mounted rubber mattress/zero-gravity sensory-deprivation chamber, or probably just in bed at home like most normal, Wi-Fi-reliant people." "You feel upon your face the soft touch of the wind/sun/rain/snow/hurricane/natural disaster of your choice." "You feel heavy, every atom of your body gently pulled down by a force just slightly greater than earth's gravitational pull of 9.8 meters per second squared, as though you were, for the sake of this analogy, atop the clouds of Saturn."

By this point, I was really sinking into a state of deep relaxation. I was starting to feel very much at one with the universe, my consciousness hazy with the fog of calm, my mind a landscape of tranquility. Then, a voice broke through the silence: "WOULD YOU LIKE TO CREATE A WEBSITE? VISIT OUR HOW-TO-CREATE-A-WEBSITE WEBSITE AT HOW-TO-CREATE-A-WEBSITE.WEBSITE AND BLAH AND BLAH AND BLAHBLAHBLAH…"

AAAGGGHHH!!! *Why are there ads on YouTube? Why are the ads on YouTube so much louder than the regular YouTube content? Click, click, click.*

Has it not been five seconds yet? How is that possible? Oh no, it's one of those video-will-play-after-seventeen-minute-ad ads. We're doomed.

Indeed, as per the original plan, much meditation did follow, but of a different kind, as I meditated upon these questions, and many like them, sleeplessly waiting for morning.

What became apparent quite quickly regarding the matter of side effects is that the question wasn't how to get rid of them, but which particular flavor of torment to choose at each given moment. When I first started receiving chemotherapy, it gave me terrible stomach cramps. To combat them, my doctor prescribed anti-cramp medication, the type that pregnant women take against Braxton-Hicks. It worked wonders, wondrously replacing the cramps with extreme nausea. The nausea medication followed, uncourteously failing to alleviate the nausea, resulting in much sleep loss. To help with the insomnia, my doctor prescribed sleeping pills, which made me drowsy during the day. I had a sneaking suspicion that the next step in this pharmaceutical production of "there once was an old lady who swallowed a fly" would be some magic drug that cures everything but causes extreme stomach cramps. By that point, I didn't really fancy going back to my doctor. Why? Well, I was afraid he would prescribe me a horse, of course.

It appeared that, like it or not, I was taking a ride on the side-effect train of consequences, and the only question was whether to follow its sickly circular route or to choose one particular station in which to be stranded.

In a way, this tireless chase after complete respite and a time when all things are all good all at the same time is the story of our lives. Infanthood, a condition characterized by worriless existence and play, fails to satisfy us, as it is accompanied by forced toy-sharing and lack of independent access to snacks. We wait impatiently for childhood, only to find out that we've replaced those minor troubles with the woes of homework and early bedtime (or so I've been told by other parents). Adolescence offers little comfort, trading those for acne and moodiness. From there on it's pretty much a roller-coaster-run of successive stresses and reliefs: marriage cures loneliness but inflicts relationship challenges; parenthood fills the void of an empty house but imposes financial burden; work replaces economic anxiety with work-related stress; old age offers rest in return for depleting health; the final stage, the only one truly free of side effects, is generally unappealing.

Unfortunately, the drug that brings about the transitions between these various states of pressure-relief payoffs is one we take involuntarily: time. Fortunately, at each and every stage, the greatest choice is present: to embrace each moment in time, with all its complexity, enjoy the good and endure the bad, or just moan a lot.

Personally, I do a bit of both, just to be on the safe side.

31
Driving the Point Home

Understanding the difference between empathy and sympathy can be hard. Infinitely harder, however, is any object that collides with your shin.

Painful Truths

"It could be worse." Of course it could. Considering the fact that there are an infinite number of various forms of pain and anguish and combinations thereof, it could, most literally, always be worse. There is, by definition, never a point of the worst possible suffering. And somehow, this multitude of actual and potential misery is supposed to be a comfort to us all.

Personally, I don't find much solace in the relativity of my suffering to that of a hypothetical and worse-off version of myself. Nor do I find relief in having been spared the sometimes-unimaginable misfortune of others. What I do occasionally find in them, however, is inspiration.

During one of our many visits to the outpatient clinic, my wife and I were sitting and waiting not so patiently for me to be summoned to the nurses' room and get hooked up (to an IV pole) with some drugs, when we heard a patient's name being called out. Our independent gazes followed the searching nurse as she walked off toward one of the bed-furnished treatment rooms and disappeared from view. Then we turned to each other slowly and silently, until our eyes met with mutual recognition. We knew that name. We knew it well. We knew it all too well. It was the name of a taxi driver we had taken a ride with fifteen years ago.

No, I don't remember the name of every person I come in contact with. Or every person I know. Or every person I'm supposed to know, for that matter. I'm quite good with my kids' names, though I do have to do that thing where you go through all of them and the dog before getting the right one. Their ages are a whole different story. How do they expect me to remember when they themselves can't seem to settle on something for any decent amount of time?

I don't remember the name of every person I come into casual and temporary contact with, because I've never *known* the names of most of them. Perhaps tragically, perhaps necessarily, and perhaps with no philosophical or muse-worthy significance at all, such encounters tend to reduce the other parties involved to the two-dimensionality of black-and-white background scenery against which we experience our narrow window of full-colored conscious existence.

I actually do have a habit of stealing a peak at a taxi driver's nameplate once settled in. I'm not fully sure why, but I think that it stems from a certain degree of paranoia, the desire to know the name of my potential kidnapper, or more likely the name of the taxi driver whose car was stolen by my potential kidnapper. No one wants the last person they ever see to be a total stranger.

But that wasn't the case here. This particular taxi driver wasn't just someone we had taken a ride with fifteen years ago. It was someone we had taken a *few* rides with fifteen years ago. We had actually grown quite fond of each other. It's not every day that your occasional taxi driver takes your family to his brother's random and improvised horse ranch that's suspiciously located in a small empty patch of land just outside the city for a complimentary gallop. With time, our friendly driver passed the taxi baton over to a friend, and, considering the fact that, after all, our relationship was taxi-ride based, we lost touch. Then we heard that he was diagnosed with cancer. We didn't contact him personally, partly because, after all, our relationship was taxi-ride based, but mainly because we're shameful people. But we did make a point of receiving periodic updates from our mutual acquaintance. He fluctuated between doing well and not doing so well and doing not so well at all, as does many a cancer patient.

Time passed, and we seldom, if ever, thought about him, until we heard his name called out by a nurse standing only a few feet away from us. Apparently, he still had cancer. Apparently, he was receiving treatment right here, right now.

Obviously, we went to find him and catch up. Ignoring someone you know has had cancer for fifteen years in a world in which the variety and quality of communication options have eliminated the significance of any form of spatial boundaries is one thing. Ignoring them a little bit longer when they're just around the corner is something else altogether. Apparently.

We didn't know what to expect. Who knew what shape he would be in and how he would look? Fifteen years of "healthy" aging under normal circumstances can often suffice to alter the appearance of a long-lost friend and provide a degree of shock upon reunion; sprinkle those years with the effects of periodic cancer and cancer treatment, and you have yourself a decent recipe for the walking dead, not to mention the not uncommon occurrence of the non-walking dead.

But we were prepared. We knew the facts: he had cancer, hardly a claim to fame in an oncology clinic, where everyone (with the exception of the doctors, nurses, administrative personnel, research coordinators, maintenance staff, volunteers, family, friends, and visitors) has cancer. We were ready for the worst. After all, what could be worse than having cancer?

Well, it turns out that there *is* something worse than cancer. The key to solving this riddle is basic arithmetic: what's worse than cancer is two cancers.

We entered the room he was in and were greeted by a ghostly shell of the man we once knew. A smiling, cheerful ghostly shell of the man we once knew. He welcomed us in warmly and expressed true delight at seeing us. We sat beside his bed as he told us how, after years of battling a type of blood cancer, a second and unrelated cancer had been discovered in his stomach. Due to its urgency, it required immediate surgery, and all other treatment had to be temporarily discontinued. The operation resulted in the removal of substantial portions of his stomach and digestive system. In the meantime, the original cancer, perhaps wanting to reclaim some of the attention it once held, made its presence known by springing into action in full force. Upon recovery from the surgery, the original treatment plan was resumed. This included daily hospital visits to receive chemotherapy and other treats.

Suffice to say, we weren't quite sure how to respond. It's a hard one to comfort, the two-cancer affliction, considering the combination of severe illness and truly bad statistical misfortune. But it became evident very quickly that we didn't need to comfort him. His attention was fully focused on us as he inquired about my health and offered words of encouragement, as though I was the patient and he was the visitor (technically, we were both "the patient" and therefore, to a certain degree, both "the visitor," but if we were to subtract the common denominator of "one cancer," he would still be a cancer patient and I wouldn't, so the point stands). When we asked how he was coping with it all, he smiled and said, "Look, every day I come into the hospital, lie in a bed, read the papers, and drink coffee. I relax and enjoy the peace and quiet. What do I have to complain about?" Well, I had a few ideas that were probably pretty good candidates for answers to that question, but I decided to keep them to myself and instead let my mind be blown away with his awe-inspiring attitude to life. No, his long and punishing trial of illness and suffering didn't make me *feel* better. It *made* me better. A better person. And he did it without even trying, and without even realizing, by virtue of suffering with dignity, but mainly by managing to find the beautiful amid the horrifying, the pleasure amid the pain.

He was "just" a guy we took a taxi ride with, not someone officially employed by the University of Life to teach a course in inspirational thinking. But we tend to forget that, to the overwhelming majority of people in the world, we're all, at best, just a guy they take a taxi ride with or the metaphorical equivalent thereof, and we should never let that fool us into forgetting just how impactful our actions can be on them, even if they're joining us on the journey of life for just a brief ride.

32

Good Mourning

I attend funerals only if I'm delivering a eulogy or I'm the subject of one.

Grave Thoughts

People are always calling me to tell me about their dead relatives.

They seem to think that I'm some sort of death expert. The weird thing is that I haven't the faintest idea who these people are. When one answers the phone and an unfamiliar voice starts going on about a recently deceased family member and asks for advice, one feels quite uncomfortable interrupting. I'm never quite sure just how long to let the solemn soliloquy go on before asking who in the world it is, and why in the world they think that I'm the universal grief directory.

At first, I thought it was some sort of bizarre cancer-club initiation procedure. "This just in, we have a new member. Get on the phones, people, tell him about your dead." But that seemed unlikely, considering how unlikely it seemed.

People do need to share, though—at least those people who need to share do. And we would be heartless to deprive them of that. On one occasion, while I was receiving treatment, my wife and I were approached by a lovely young man who had recently started volunteering in oncology wards, doing rounds, initiating conversations with patients and family members, sympathizing and keeping spirits high, giving people an outlet to unburden, and making sure that no one was alone and miserable. A fine and noble initiative no doubt, the sort that truly kindhearted folk undertake, leaving the rest of us with a warm and pleasant feeling and hope for mankind.

He sat beside us and introduced himself, explaining his new role and goal. He started by telling us a bit about himself and what brought him there. His two-year-old son had been born with cancer (yes, I, too, learned something new and terrifying that day), and had been in treatment since, including the removal of a kidney. He was a strong boy and was doing well, but obviously it was extremely challenging, both physically and emotionally, for everyone involved. Still, this optimistic father was in fine spirits, and appeared to be coping in an admirable and healthy manner.

He spoke for an hour.

Forget about *my* life, I couldn't even comment on *his* story, he didn't let me get a word in edgewise. Every question was, apparently, rhetorical, and every detail was followed by ten more of varied levels of un-relatedness. "Oh, dear," he exclaimed at some point, "is that the time? I must move on to the next patient. There are lots of people here today and I have plenty of work to do. Please feel free to call me if you ever need to listen, I'm always available. All the best. Anyway, it's been lovely talking to you, Mr., er, what did you say your name was? Oh, you didn't, did you, that's right, I didn't give you a chance to. Goodbye."

But it's OK, I'm not much of a sharer anyway (with the small notable exception of this book), but I'm a decent listener, and if I can be of service to a brother-in-harms, then that's the proper thing to do. We all have different needs. It's not a matter of being secretive; it's just that while some people have a need to share a burden, for others sharing *is* a burden.

Soon after my diagnosis, upon recommendation and against my natural inclination, I joined a multiple myeloma association, a supportive network of sorts. I went along with it because it really only involved being committed to two things: ignoring the quarterly newsletters, and not showing up to the group gatherings, and I thought I would probably be able to manage those tasks. They call me occasionally to ask if I'll be attending a forthcoming event, and I say no—then I feel guilty for a while. Sometimes I get the impression that they fall a bit short on their quota of ill people (or people who are ill enough to belong but well enough to attend) and that the meetings are under-attended, which is a strange thing to feel bad about. People just don't have the decency to be ill these days. I can't unsubscribe, though. That would imply that I've either been cured or have died, the former being a medical miracle and the latter a lie that's probably quite hard to maintain.

Another time, I was approached by someone who was putting together a local workshop focusing on restoring hope. I informed the organizers that there must have been some confusion and the hope they found must be someone else's, since, as far as I was aware, I hadn't lost mine.

That's just the way it is. Some people are quite fine just getting on with their own little story, not needing to share and compare, laugh and cry together. And some people need to call a total stranger and tell them about their dead relatives.

In the end, it turned out that my mysterious postmortem phone phenomenon had quite a simple explanation. It's all in the small details, really. Some people get phone calls inquiring about pizza or dry cleaning; others are on the receiving end of various other misdialings. It's just a matter of having the right wrong number. It turns out that my phone number differs by a single digit from that of the author of a very popular *hilchos aveilus sefer*, who generously shared his/my number on the front page of his book and frequently receives (and sometimes, apparently, doesn't receive) calls from advice-seeking mourners. Calls with pressing questions such as, I imagine, "Hello, Rabbi. I wanted to ask what happens if my cousin's cousin [wait, isn't that you?] died on Erev Shabbos that fell on a Tuesday on a leap year—is it OK to serve cheese bourekas at the yahrzeit, or is that a problem?" Or, in my case, more like, "Oh, I'm sorry. Are you not Rabbi so-and-so, author of such-and-such?"

"Actually, no. It so happens that I'm not. Unless I'm an exceptionally prolific and obliviously published sleep-writer, that is, in which case you should probably call me later once I'm asleep and I'll try to help. Sorry, mate, wrong number. If you really need to share, I can spare you a few minutes, but no more than two hours, *ad meah v'esrim*. The best thing would be to try calling a bit later in the day. I've never really been much of a mourning person."

33
Save the Date

Men are from Mars. That's probably why every time I think I have a good idea my wife snickers.

Universal Truths

A guy from Mars and a girl from Venus set up a date. The guy comes to pick her up 243 days early because he forgets to take the two planets' different rotation speeds into account. He then gets severe burns traveling through the sulfuric acid clouds. When he finally lands, he finds out that his trendy new sweater isn't suitable for the local temperature of 900°F. Funny? Not particularly. But informative.

Science Isn't a Joke, p. 1

They say that absence makes the heart grow fonder. Rubbish. It's chips and onion rings, with a dash of sweet chili sauce. They say that happiness is when what you think, what you say, and what you do are in harmony. Rubbish. It's chips and onion rings, with a dash of sweet chili sauce. They say that the key to a healthy relationship is communication. That one is probably true.

There are two ways to look at chemotherapy. You can see it as a burden, or you can see it as a date. When my wife and I were faced with this unchoice reality, we already had plenty of burdens, so we opted to treat treatment as a treat. We had been married for fifteen years and had thirteen years' worth of children. The last time we had been out for a romantic dinner was on our wedding night, if we can stretch the definition of "romantic" to include an event in which you have no privacy and "dinner" to one in which you don't eat. As is the case with so many people, life was happening to us, and it was happening fast. Too fast to stop and think about what we could and what we should. Too fast to think about anything, really, not daring to loosen our grip on the rat race of routine, lest we fall off from the sheer force of Earth's perpetual spin. The thought of taking a break from life, work, and the children, two mornings a week, and officially scheduling a whole half-day of doing absolutely nothing, together, was a madman's notion. But crazy things tend to happen when crazy things happen to you.

Don't mistake me for an optimist. I'm not one to ignore the empty half of the glass. How can I? It's right there on top of the full half. But I try to look past it, too, at the full half, and not to be too much of a pessimist. There are times when one needs to be a pragmatist and just get a smaller cup. It's the only way to have a full cup no matter how little water life gives you. Adaptation is the key to happiness. Dale Carnegie knew what he was talking about when he said: "Success is getting what you want; happiness is wanting what you get." Or maybe he didn't. I think there's a chance that he was too busy making friends and influencing people to stop worrying and start living and produce accurate and realistic witticisms. I don't believe that anyone "wants" what they get, unless they got what they wanted, and even then, it's rare to still want it after you have it, since one is usually too busy wanting the next thing. "Wanting" is simply too strong a word. "Coming to terms with." "Accepting." "Being content with." Those are within reach, without a total distortion of our emotional wiring. "Spinning a fun twist on" is also somewhere out there, and that should surely be one of our goals. So let it be said: "Success is getting what you want; happiness is coming to terms with, accepting, being content with, and hoping to spin a fun twist on what you get." Granted, it's not as catchy, but not everything catchy is necessarily good, a point aptly demonstrated by many a virus. Better an unpolished real pearl of wisdom than a shiny fake one.

And so it became our semiweekly routine: rise early, get the kids out, travel to the hospital, summon the lift, wait for the lift, press the button again, wait a bit more, consider the stairs, reconsider, take the lift, arrive in the outpatient clinic, wait, get pricked in the arm and injected in the stomach, sit for three to six hours, watch strange people walk by, unhook the IV, and finally, culminate the day in the food court of the adjacent mall over onion rings and chips and a breathtaking mountain-range view. With a dash of sweet chili sauce. And somehow, it made it all worth it.

Then, one day, my world went dark. I was told that my immune system had reached a point low enough to require avoiding fast food and people. I was grateful to my white blood cells (or lack thereof) for the people prohibition, but the fast-food ban posed a serious problem. What would be of our custom? What would sweeten our days?

Well, it turns out that if you sneak out of the clinic with your IV pole and a paper mask on for disguise (and protection), and you don't mind attracting a few suspicious glances as you walk through a mall, they actually will serve you at the burger place, no questions asked. Granted, scoffing down onion rings and chips through a paper mask was a bit of a challenge, not to mention a death wish, but tradition is very important and sometimes we have to go out of our way to preserve it, if not ourselves.

Several years have passed since then, and in a strange and confusing way, I really miss those days. I guess that means we really did manage to fill our cup after all, together with our plates.

34
Looking Forward

The question isn't if there is life after death for mankind, but if there was life before death for man.

M.E.

So, what does the future hold? Who knows. Well, technically, my doctor does, and by "my doctor" I mean everything we know about multiple myeloma and its treatments at this point in time, based on the experiences of hundreds of thousands of patients worldwide. The relapse rate is somewhere in the area of 100 percent. Of course, it's important not to have a bleak perspective, and also to know how to analyze statistics. Many patients indeed do not experience a relapse. But that's because they die from other causes before they have the chance. There are others who won't experience a relapse because they'll never have a remission in the first place and will ultimately die while in their first and only bout, soon after their diagnosis or many years later. How's that for bleak?

But it's alright, that's just the way it is—some cancers are chronic. They're still preferable to their terminal counterparts. Also chronic is the capacity for laughter.

And if statistics are already on the table, who knows, it's not beyond the realm of possible that I might end up being a one-in-a-million myeloma patient who experiences only one occurrence and lives a cancer-free life ever after. In my eyes, however, hanging my hopes on an unrealistic and negligible probability that is bound to lead to disappointment isn't a wise choice. I'd rather put it this way: there's a 99.999 percent chance that I'll have some more stories to tell. Worse things have happened.

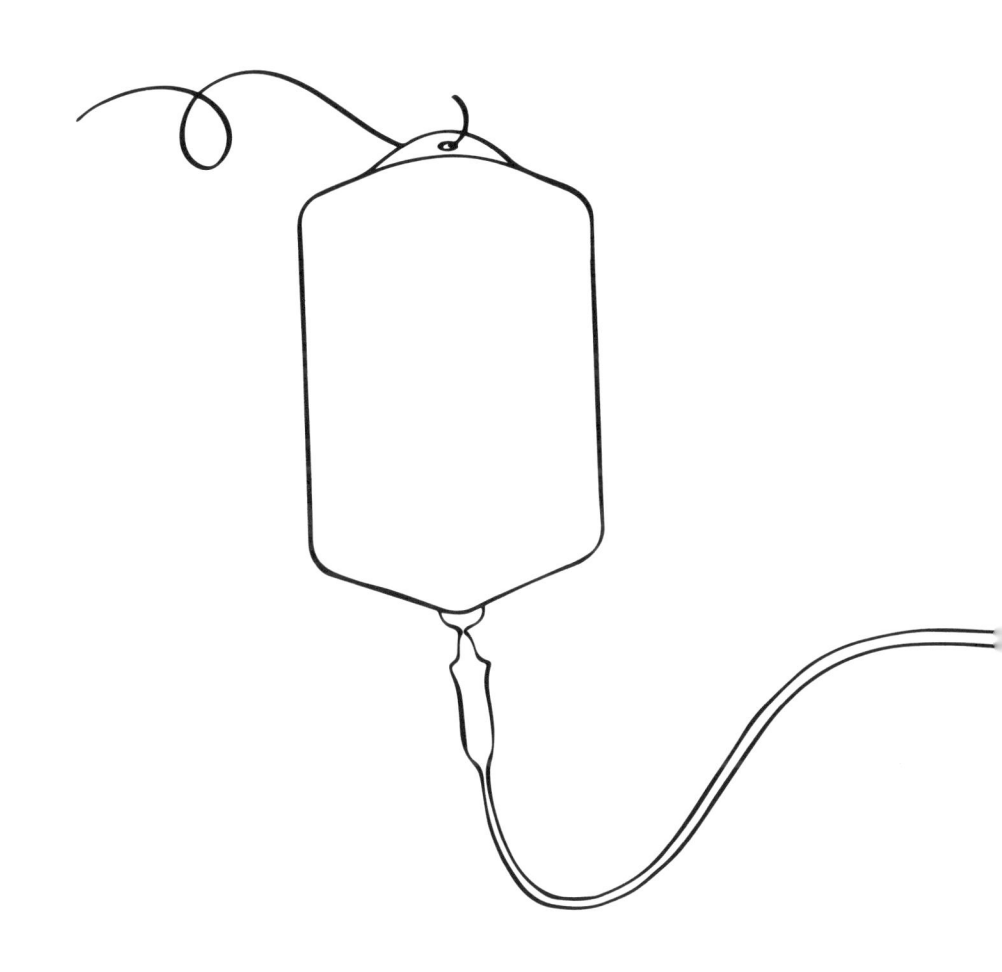

Part Two

35
The Show Must Go On. And On. And On.

All the world's a stage, and all the men and women merely players desperately trying to rewrite their script in the hope of finding a better play to star in. But no matter how hard you try, it will never be exactly as you like it.

Quilliam Shakespeare

Five years later.

Well, not five years since writing all of the above. But five years, to the year, after the last treatment of round one, came round two.

Since I was, obviously, secretly hoping to defy the odds and be well forever, when the time came, I suddenly felt that the five-year break I'd "enjoyed" was very short. Upon my return to the hospital, however, I was informed that this was actually considered quite a decent stretch considering I was without any treatment, not even "maintenance" (a term that never fails to evoke a mental image of a doctor tightening a patient's bolts and oiling his joints). But just as I was starting to develop a deep sense of pride for my body for its impressive half-decade of resilience, I realized that essentially what this meant was that, looking ahead, a similar-length hiatus would be considered extremely fortunate, and highly unlikely. I hadn't yet even had a chance to fully appreciate just how disappointing the sequel was when I already had to start worrying about facing the impending doom of an inevitable (and entirely unnecessary) third installment.

I had known all along that my drama was to unfold as a series and not a standalone feature film, but knowing and *knowing* are two very different things. With the arrival of my long "anticipated" new episode, it began to sink in that the next season, which had long been commissioned, was already in advanced stages of production. Granted, at this point I was only confronted with one entirely predictable new development. But it felt like the full plot, with all its future recurring, repetitive, miserable potential, was tumbling in all at once.

It was a show called *Cancer 2.0—Back with a Vengeance*, and it was time to binge.

36
Survivors' Guild

I see no reason to limit myself: I regret both what I have done and what I haven't.

Miss A. Tributed

Unfortunately, time wasn't the only thing that passed in the interval between the first and second rounds of my match against cancer, mortality's second-ranked opponent.[1] This five-year period also saw the untimely passing of several individuals who were less fortunate than me in their encounter with the illness, which in their case graduated from dreadly to deadly. The list includes an uncle, a former employer, a high school classmate, a yeshiva *shiur*-mate, and a student in her early twenties. (I am inclined, almost beyond control, to preface the latter with "most tragic of all," but refrain, against my own judgment, and hopefully not sinfully, from doing so. Can one honestly classify any one such occurrence as definitively more tragic than another? Can we really claim that a parent leaving behind a young child is objectively and categorically more tragic than a child leaving behind a young parent, or vice versa? The only thing that can be said with a degree of certainty is

---

[1] To totally defeat the purpose of this (attempted) curiosity-inducing wording and save you the googling, the answer is heart disease. And still, somehow, the C words "chocolate," "cake," "cookies," "crisps/chips," "candy," "cream cheese," and even "cardiovascular" don't have the same effect.

that to be able to answer that question would be a greater tragedy than either, and that the "ability" of some to answer such questions on behalf of others is perhaps the greatest tragedy of all.)

With the arrival of each new departure, I found myself time and time again doubting the appropriateness of my endeavor—incorporating humor into writing about my own experiences (or, some might say, incorporating my experiences into writing about my own humor). This was especially so since my cancer is only chronic while for so many others out there the condition is terminal. My condition may be forever, but at least I *have* a forever. With each such occurrence I made a final and irrevocable decision to scrap the project. What right did I have to write, and with lightheartedness no less, as though I were an insider, when clearly our experiences were smiles apart. I would picture the deceased standing around me as I wrote, an audience to my creative labor, peering over my shoulder at my computer screen, criticizing both the content and the very concept of my enterprise.

I should clarify that I'm not referring to some sort of survivor's guilt. This is for two simple reasons: "survivor," and "guilt." I'm not a survivor, and I feel no guilt. Not in general, of course; I feel plenty of guilt, mostly regarding things that don't warrant it. After all, it's our cultural heritage. The well-known tidbit stating that the Inuit have twenty/fifty/ten million words to describe various types of snow, as a result of (or resulting in) their perception of a precipitation that is so central to their everyday life, is very likely, at least partially, and perhaps disappointingly, mythical. A better candidate to represent the phenomenon of "linguistic relativity," whatever we are to make of it, would be the abundance of Hebrew terms for variations of sins (may they be whitened as snow), accountability, and guilt. To be honest, I should probably have done proper comparative research before making such an assertion. I suspect, however, that if I did, I would readily find a unique term for the specific sin of "maintaining a slacken attitude toward philological research while incorporating an almost intangibly related side point into an unauthoritative document."

So, no, guilt is not in short supply; it's just currently unavailable in the survivor department of this particular branch. Which brings us back to point one, keeping us neatly in the language district. "Survivor." My intention is not, in this particular instance, to challenge the dictionary definition or the common uses of the word, merely to state my personal sentiment: I am not a survivor, I'm just still alive (a "still-aliver," if you wish). If pressed for clarification, I doubt I would be able to provide a precise formula describing the exact nature and degree of threat or suchlike factors that determine the "proper" use of the term, though I imagine that a minimal requirement would be the existence of a sentient aggressor. Frankly, what it boils down to, is that placing myself in the same category as victims of the Holocaust and abuse seems, to me, demeaning to their particular unimaginable and hellish form of suffering. It goes without saying, of course, that other patients are absolutely free to assert otherwise; it's entirely their bad choice.

If not guilt, then what was the hitch? Why stop writing? It was quite simple. At those times it seemed abundantly and undeniably clear that there is absolutely nothing, not one single thing, funny about this whole business. I'm as big a fan of witticisms and quote-worthy quips as the next guy (assuming that he's a fan), but with all due indifference, when George Bernard Shaw's doctor said that "life does not cease to be funny when people die any more than it ceases to be serious when people laugh," he was speaking absolute nonsense (unless, of course, what he actually meant is what I'm about to say, in which case he was clearly deeply wise).

This was always the first stage. Before long, I would progress to a second stage, in which I would reason that perhaps there *is* room for humor, but that room is, and should remain, under lock and key inside my mind palace. Later, I would move on to another stage, which involved being open to the idea that it is entirely possible and indeed plausible that some other people might find the lighter sides of one's medical experiences entertaining, while maintaining that to voice such sentiments would be disrespectful to the memory of the late and the ongoing experiences of the living and their kin.

And thus, the repeat of each such cycle would hamper both my will and ability to continue what might be seen as whitewashing a difficult and unpleasant matter.

But time and time again, without fail, after each occurrence, I would at some point advance to stage four. I would run into someone who had read earlier drafts of the book and found it entertaining, entirely appropriate, and, not insignificantly, encouraging and uplifting. I would be asked how one could get hold of a copy "for someone I know," because everyone knows someone to whom the subject is relevant, which ultimately means that it is relevant to everyone.

I feared being seen as disrespectful, but my intentions are and have always been not to make light of a serious subject, but to bring light into a dark one, into the lives of those who are experiencing it, and those who are experiencing others experiencing it. I sincerely hope that in the pages that follow I will manage to (continue to) do exactly that.

And to potential readers who may, despite the above attempted justification, find my writing difficult to digest, I pose one simple question: How in the world have you made it this far?

37
Writing Has No Wry

Why did you write this book?

No One

No one, at any point, asked me why I actually wrote this book. Perhaps it's obvious to everyone. If that's the case, I'm incredibly impressed and equally curious, since it certainly wasn't, and still isn't, obvious to me. Was it to entertain? To inform? To guide? To console? To instill hope? Was it primarily a personal exercise to help myself process what I had been through? Was it all of the above, or none of the above? On some level, I did what we all do when faced with a multiple-choice question we don't know the answer to: point to the big C and hope no one asks for an explanation.

In the previous chapter, I highlighted the potential benefits this book may have for others. That's definitely not the worst excuse for writing a book. I won't pretend, however, that my motives were exclusively altruistic. At the risk of further wearing out an already threadbare cliché, the writing process was intended, hopefully, to be therapeutic. In what way, exactly, I wasn't sure; it was more of a natural urge than a calculated purge.

While in treatment, I didn't really feel that I needed help. I'm sure some would say that this was an indication of just how much help I needed; not only did I need help, I also needed help realizing that I needed help, and I probably needed help with that, too. But as far as I was concerned, I was absolutely fine. This was certainly my state of mind when, on the first day of my month-long stay in the hospital, I was visited by the ward therapist, a young man perfectly suited to be the poster boy for therapy itself, from the trendy, thick-rimmed glasses and cardigan down to the "and how does that make you feel" print on his T-shirt. I wasn't made aware in advance that this was a service I was expected to provide, and I wasn't quite sure how to politely turn down his implicit offer to fix all my life issues in one casual bedside meeting. To his T-shirt I responded, "Nauseous, mainly," and to "In your opinion, what would make the problem better?" I answered, "Chemotherapy, probably."

"How much quality time do you spend with your loved ones?" followed, meriting my "At this particular moment, less than I would like to."

"What things do you find difficult?" prompted "Ending conversations," and it would have been nothing short of a crime against the concept of humor itself not to reply to "What keeps you up at night?" with "Insomnia." The impromptu session came to its natural conclusion when "What kinds of situations make you feel uncomfortable?" was met with the silence that served both as an answer and a real-time demonstration.

On another occasion, while spending the day in the outpatient clinic, I was paid a visit by the ward psychiatrist, an older lady (older than who?), who sat with us for a few minutes. Not an entirely unwelcome break from the monotony of a long day sitting idly, but once again not an avenue I was looking to explore at that point in time or ever. After we had spoken for a few minutes, as she got up to leave, she told us that she was severely visually impaired, and that we shouldn't take offense if, over the course of our future visits to the hospital, when we cross paths in the hallways, she doesn't acknowledge us. Now, I'm not saying that I was glad to learn of her eye condition, but the implications for working on avoidance behavior were obvious, and let's just say that that was the last she saw of us.

But once the fifteen months of treatment were over, I suddenly felt an overwhelming sense of emptiness fill me. I imagine it had something to do with being distracted while busy receiving treatment—a time-consuming, attention-guzzling, emotional-space-devouring activity. I won't go as far as saying that I was fighting for my life and my body kicked into emergency mode, sending adrenaline coursing through my veins and temporarily dulling any sense of pain and fear (though I do like the idea of a battle that can be fought from bed while sipping coffee and reading a book). But I certainly was, if nothing else, occupied with taking care of something urgent, which didn't leave much time and opportunity to stop, think, and process. I also imagine that had I made even minimal use of my short time with the ward-wandering counselor instead of snappily exercising my passive-aggression reflexes, I might have been somewhat prepared for this highly unsurprising development.

But the truth is that it was much more than just a matter of no longer being distracted. It was something deeper, more fundamental to my very being. For the duration of the treatment, being a cancer patient was what I did (for a living, one might say). Its absence, rather than restoring calm and stability, left behind a void: a treatment-shaped hole not only in my schedule, but in my self. I won't go as far as saying that it felt like losing a sense of who I was or losing a friend (though I do like the idea of a friend who appears at times of need and cures cancer), but it wasn't entirely unlike losing a meaningful job, a gratifying position, or a really nice pancake recipe.

This newfound emptiness didn't last long, however. That's a good thing, in theory, if it wasn't for the fact that what it began filling itself with was a cascade of traumatic memories, memories of various experiences from the past year or so, things that at the time hadn't even seemed to be particularly bad. It was strange to me that my remembering self was having a harder time coping than my experiencing self originally had. Time was meant to heal, not reveal. But I guess that when you combine an absence of distraction with a loss of sense of purpose, you can expect a bit of trauma—heavy as it may be—to rise to the surface.

I began by compiling a list of some of the (surprisingly) entertaining incidents that had occurred during the course of the diagnosis and treatment and used them as starting points to tell the story. I was able to summon up many of the experiences to memory, but most popped into my mind at random over time once I started the process, often while commuting on public transport and unable to put the thoughts into writing properly. On these occasions, I either scribbled down a few semi-intelligible words on a scrap of paper or spoke in hushed and mumbled tones into my phone to record a memo to myself. In most cases I later managed to decipher these cryptic codes, though I still hope one day to figure out what precious literary gem is hidden in the message "blood, magic, science, seashell."

What I ultimately discovered was that by highlighting the lighter side of things, the memories of the humorous and pleasant aspects were strengthened, and many of the experiences were reframed as being largely positive. I had not rewritten my story, but had certainly illustrated it in a way that made remembering it a much more enjoyable experience.

I'm not quite sure if this is how writing is meant to be therapeutic. I am quite sure that if I asked the cancer-county counselor, he would refer to page one of the manual and say, "There's no right or wrong way to do it; it's whatever works best for *you*," and be proud of me for how far I've come. As for the ward psychiatrist, well, if she could only see me now.

APPENDIX—BLOOD, MAGIC, SCIENCE, SEASHELL

Somewhere between writing and rewriting and reading and rereading this chapter, I believe I may have cracked this unintended code.

Physicist Richard Feynman was once told by an artist friend that his scientific approach to nature robs it of all beauty. From an artist's perspective, claimed the artist, a flower is beautiful. But by viewing it from the perspective of its biological components, scientists take it apart and render it dull. The professor responded that on the contrary, as a scientist he sees, in addition to the aesthetic beauty available to everyone, many additional layers of beauty: the inner structure, the complexity on the cellular level, the various processes that take place within the organism, and the interaction with the insects that pollinate it, all adding to the excitement, mystery, and awe of the flower.

In a similar vein I pondered the following. I remember being told as a child, as I'm sure many others were, that the sound you hear when putting a large seashell or conch to your ear is the sound of the ocean. The question of how exactly this sound was trapped in or transported via the shell, and how it also makes its way into all cups, bowls, and the palms of your hands, was never properly addressed, as is often the case with such fantastical traditions. Exactly why "we" perpetuate this nonsense is unclear. I imagine it's a stubborn remnant of an outdated instruction manual, the same one that encourages telling young children that a vaguely defined, female, winged entity will creep into their room while they're asleep and take their teeth (hopefully only the already detached ones), for some undisclosed and inevitably disturbing use, instead of cutting out the middle-fairy and taking credit for the gift ourselves, and perhaps saying something soothing like, "I'm sure losing that tooth must have been uncomfortable and a little scary. You've been so brave, here's a little treat. Don't use it to buy something that will rot your teeth; when this set falls out, even the tooth fairy won't be able to help you."

Those of us who, upon realizing that seashells are unlikely to carry anything into our ear other than ten thousand strains of bacteria, have done some minimal research, will know that what you hear when you put one to your ear is the same thing you hear when you don't put one to your ear, just louder—certain frequencies of the ambient noise amplified (which means that technically, the sound you hear in a seashell is indeed the sea, provided that you happen to be by the sea). There was a theory that what you heard was the sound of the blood flowing through the blood vessels in your ear, but apparently this is not the case, as increase in heart rate does not affect the sound, and in a soundproofed room, with no background noise to amplify, shells are completely silent.

And here's the question: is seashell resonance (to give it its grown-up name) any less magical now that we've taken the sea out of the shell? The answer, at least for me, is a resounding no. It's so much better, and more magical. Sound waves, frequencies, reverberation, and the mechanics of hearing are far more fascinating than an imaginary long-distance phone call from the ocean. God's creation is more amazing, exciting, and awe-inspiring than any fantasy we can conjure up in our minds. If creativity is what we're looking for, we need look no further than creation itself, in all its grandeur, vastness, and detail. *Mah rabu, gadlu, v'katnu maasecha Hashem.*

Having successfully deciphered the code and figuring out what I meant, one question remains: Why? Why did I think any of this was relevant to the book? I guess the world does contain some true wonders after all.

38
Trial and Terror

They say the biggest risk is not taking any risks, and the biggest mistake is being afraid of making mistakes. I say the biggest risk and biggest mistake is living by inspirational quotes.

M.T. Wordsworth-Nothing

To take part in a clinical trial, or not to take part in a clinical trial, that is the question.

In some dire cases, when the experimental drug is the only viable remaining option, this is basically the same question as the original "to be or not to be." In a sense, that can be an easier decision to make, though by no means an easy one. But with the ever-increasing abundance of experimental drugs and clinical research trials available for a wide variety of conditions, for many this is quite an undramatic option that presents itself, or is presented, at various stages of treatment. In these cases, lacking a sense of urgency, the decision becomes somewhat difficult to make, as the pros and cons are often not particularly substantially overwhelming.

I had decided not to participate in a clinical trial during my first encounter with the illness, but that was in large because it involved a chance of receiving a placebo. In round two, I was presented with the option of taking part in a trial with a new and promising drug that allegedly offered better results and milder side effects and also wasn't made of starch and sugar and trickery. A dream drug, by the sound of it, if your idea of a dream is having cancer and getting excited about discovering a new type of poison that kills slightly fewer healthy cells than other poisons available on the market.

Pros and cons? Aside from the trifling matter of possibly receiving the most effective drug available at the moment, the benefits of taking part in the trial were the increased testing and the added supervision. The downsides were the increased testing and the added supervision, which involved longer and more frequent visits, periodically filling in questionnaires, and waiting for approval before, during, and after each treatment.

A built-in feature of clinical trials is the services of a research coordinator who, I was told, would be in charge of scheduling the various necessary appointments and dealing with much of the bureaucracy that naturally accompanies hospital visits. The coordinator would also be the contact person for all test results and information. This sounded like a promising prospect and was a significant factor in ultimately making my decision to take part in the trial.

And indeed, it proved to be very helpful. Within a short time, we developed a pretty consistent routine: She would make the appointment. I would arrive. I would wait to be seen by a nurse. She would come to collect the test samples. I would wait for the initial blood results. After about an hour I would get impatient and contact her to see if there was any news. She would check and get back to me. Once the initial results arrived, she would inform me and tell me to take the steroids. Then I would wait for the biochemistry results to come in. After about an hour I would get impatient and contact her to see if there was any news. She would check and get back to me. Once the full results were in, she would inform me that she had ordered the drug from the hospital pharmacy. I would wait. After about an hour, I would get impatient and contact her to see if there was any news. She would check and say that she didn't know why it was taking such a long time. The treatment would arrive. She would remind me to put in eye drops, and then bring the ice pack eye-mask that probably did nothing other than cause great discomfort and make me look like the world's lowest-budget superhero. I would receive the treatment. She would bring the tablet for me to fill in the survey questions. At some point, the fun would be over and I would go home.

All in all, I was very grateful for all the assistance, and I decided, well in advance, that it would be a nice gesture to buy her a gift at the end of the trial. I came up with a cute idea—a personalized mug featuring all the messages that had become part of the standard routine: "You can take the steroids now"; "Waiting for biochemistry"; "I've ordered the treatment"; "Don't forget eye drops"; "Who are you, again?"; and without fail: "How much do you weigh today?" (The persistent inquiry about my weight, a nurse explained, was because if I lost 10 percent of my body weight, we would have to lower the dose of the medication accordingly. "Good lady," I said, "if I lose 10 percent of my body weight, there'll be nothing left of me." I was quite pleased with myself for that one, but she seemed to be concerned about the math and retorted, "I'm not sure you fully understand the concept of a percentage." "I think you'll find," I responded bitterly, in the safe confines of my mind, "that I'm about 100 percent sure that you don't fully understand the concept of a joke.")

Throughout the long months of treatment, I mulled over the mug idea and thought of different items I could add to the design, providing I could find a shop that prints small and strange text on items without asking too many questions. As far as treatment coordination was concerned, we were on track, the routine was running, and everything was going "smoothly" and according to plan.

I should have known it wouldn't last.

To be entirely honest, it was really all my fault. I'm just too nice, another chronic condition I suffer from. Much like my cancer and hemophilia, it's in my blood, and there's not much I can do about it.

It started quite innocuously. "I'm having a really crazy day. I have a lot of patients today, and it's going to be hard for me to go to the eye clinic and schedule your next appointment. Would you terribly mind doing it yourself just this one time?" It wasn't long before I found myself regularly weaving through maze-like narrow corridors deep in the bowels of the hospital's underground floors carrying a biohazard bag full of blood samples to the lab. One favor led to another, and before long I was doing so much self-coordinating that things became almost comical, to the point that my doctor commented (jokingly, unfortunately) that I should be receiving a salary from the hospital. But I accepted my fate, not for the first time, and probably not for the last, either. Life went on, the treatments continued, and I saw things through.

I bought the mug at the end of the trial. For myself, of course. I figured I had earned it, and thought it was a very nice gesture indeed.

L'chayim, and three cheers to me.

39
A Bumpy Start

Sometimes dreams do come true. We call these "nightmares."

Traum Trauma, vol. 1, p. 60

Things didn't get off to a great start.
It was the first day of treatment in my second bout with cancer. I was nervous about the new and experimental drug and the prediction of unpredictable side effects. What I wasn't expecting was for the trouble to begin before the treatment had even started.

After the customary hours upon hours of tests and waiting for results and waiting for the medication to arrive, all the while sitting on the hospital bed, raising and lowering it electrically and trying to remember as many songs as possible featuring the words "up" and "down," the nurse finally hooked me up to an IV that was connected to two bags—saline and steroids—opened the valves, and set the dripping in motion.

Something felt wrong immediately. There was a mounting pressure under the skin of my forearm, where the needle had been inserted, and, before my very eyes, a swelling began. Within seconds, there was a raised mound about the size of a plum, and before you ask, "Well, how big was this analogical plum?" it, too, was the size of a plum. The skin was stretched tight, and the surrounding area was not particularly comfortable, but at this point I wasn't so much focused on the pain as much as on the absolute horror of what was unfolding (or inflating) before me. There was only one thought in my mind: what happens if the swelling continues to increase at this rate? By the time I'd had that thought, the bloated bulge was the size of a peach, and before you ask, "Well, how big was this analogical peach?" it was slightly bigger than the plum from the previous analogy.

You know that things are bad when the nurse exclaims something you can't repeat in writing and runs off to tag someone else in. Before rushing off to my rescue, she closed one of the valves, but in her hurry she left the other one dripping. I now sat, terrified, my eyes fixed on my arm as the peach fast developed into a bigger peach.

Even in my panicked state, I figured that stopping the drip was the right thing to do, though at moments like this, simple logic isn't always the most reliable tool. I reasoned that, although I might get into trouble for taking matters into my own hands and meddling with the equipment, I had to do it, and quickly, while I still had hands to take matters into. I rolled down the clamp to block the flow, and the swelling stopped, though it took several minutes for the fluid to drain and be absorbed into wherever it is that fluids are absorbed into in such a case. Uncremoniously, treatment was resumed, this time in my other arm, the one not containing any fruit, literal or otherwise.

Thank God, I don't think any serious harm was done. The area is at times sensitive to the touch, mostly when the touch is forceful. Perhaps there's some trauma, too; sometimes, when I close my eyes, the image of the ballooned lump is right there in front of me. And sometimes it's still there when I open them, if I happen to be looking at the picture I took after the urgency, but not the bulge, had fully subsided. And I'll probably avoid using that vein for future infusions for the rest of my life. But, otherwise, everything seems fine.

The whole experience was far from pleasant, but I learned a few valuable lessons that day:

- Sometimes you need to go with your intuition. But it's also important to keep in mind that sometimes you shouldn't. In each given situation there's no real way to determine if you should or shouldn't go with your intuition, and you need to make that call based on intuition.

- It's important to stay calm in high-stress situations. Except for when you need to panic in order to get the job done. If you're in doubt whether you should stay calm or panic, try to stay calm long enough to figure out if you should stay calm or panic.
- Sometimes it's not a terrible thing if things go wrong early on, because, as a result, a lot of what follows might be mild by comparison. I wouldn't go as far as saying that relative to worse, bad is good, but bad is certainly better than worse, and it's always better when things are better. Of course, it's also possible that things will get worse, so don't get too excited when something bad happens.

For better or worse, we were off to a bumpy start, and in all likelihood, it was going to be a bumpy ride, with plenty of bumps in the road. All I could do about it was slow down, buckle up, strap in, chill out, and brace for impact. And, of course, try to enjoy the scenery along the way.

40
Side Notes

What goes down must come up.

Caasi Notwen

When I was given a second chance at having cancer, I decided that this time I would be better at it. One grand idea was to try and be more organized about keeping tabs on the side effects of the medications and monitoring the various aches and pains that would inevitably accompany me throughout my long period of treatment. This would surely be highly valuable information, I reasoned, on two accounts: on a personal level, it would help me identify the specific impact each part of the treatment had on my body and thus be better equipped to address the side effects; on a global level, I would be able to make a significant contribution to the ongoing research surrounding the trial drug I was receiving. As it was, I was scheduled to fill out a number of questionnaires regularly throughout the clinical trial, covering a variety of critical issues such as "On a scale of 1 to 10, with 1 being the lowest and 10 being the highest, or the other way around, how would you rate your level of dissatisfaction with this question?" and "Based on how you feel today, if you were asked last week how you felt two weeks ago, how would that make you feel?" But, obviously, what the world really needed was real, raw data from my everyday experience.

I set to work straightaway, documenting the dates and times of each treatment and the respective torments that followed, in intricate detail, effectively creating an odd journal that was both intensely boring and deeply miserable in equal measures, with riveting entries such as "arrived home, 17:30, no reactions" and "tired all the time, very nauseous, nothing new" (strangely, taken from two consecutive days).

Applying myself to the task with diligence and determination, I started amassing an impressive amount of information, priceless gems of medical knowledge. I was precise and methodical in my documentation of the events and their subsequent consequences.

This lasted two weeks.

Looking back, I'm not entirely sure if I should be disappointed with myself for giving up on my attempt to help myself so soon, or proud of myself for not sustaining my delusion of helping others any longer.

The project didn't just fizzle out due to the natural tendency of all things to collapse into chaos. There was also a eureka moment (though this moment would be the equivalent of Archimedes working hard in his study to find a way of determining the volume of gold and suddenly realizing that it was all a waste of time and throwing away the crown). The eureka moment involved déjà vu.[1] One day, staring down at my scribbly notes, I was struck by a strong sense of familiarity: I had definitely done this before. But when?

I soon remembered. It was the day of our firstborn's birth. We were told that when things kick off, we should pay attention to how long the contractions lasted and how far apart they were. In the panic of inexperience, I took this task a little bit too seriously and feverishly scrawled down the vital information on a small sticky note, thinking in my naivete that when we burst through the doors of the maternity ward I would dramatically and heroically hand it to the doctor and say, "Don't worry, I have everything you need right here."

Twenty years and six kids later, but apparently not much the wiser, here I was, scribbling again. After giving the matter some thought, I decided that, in all likelihood, information regarding the number of times

---

1 Excessive use of foreign phrases, an à la mode leitmotif employed en masse, ad nauseam, and apropos of nothing in certain genres by pseudo-intellectual language aficionados, is very much terra incognita for me, and certainly not my way of doing things.

I vomited on a Tuesday would have very little impact on future world suffering as a whole, and that my attempt to reduce my own suffering in the present was almost certainly a fool's errand. There was really no reason to continue, I reasoned. So I didn't.

It's amazing how easy it is to come up with good reasons to give up on something. The path to laziness is often paved with good arguments. As it turns out, in its very failure, my short-lived journal did provide some valuable information after all: without constant work, even the best of plans is doomed to fail. Not to mention most of our actual plans, which, let's be honest, are usually not that great to begin with.

41
Learn and Live

Blessed is the man who always fears. This, I imagine, is why I'm so utterly and completely blessed.

Mishlei Emmett 28:14

Dealing with a serious illness is difficult. Dealing with a serious illness alone is more than just difficult; it's unimaginable.

It's a good thing I didn't have to.

Many patients are fortunate enough to have a good support system of family and friends. These caring individuals provide all sorts of help: help with food, help with the kids, help with rides, and emotional support. But there's another type of help that people are kind enough to offer, a whole different category of assistance: spiritual help. Or, to be accurate, physical help achieved through spiritual means. This comes mainly in the form of davening and learning.

Personally, I've never been comfortable with the idea of people davening for my *refuah*. The request, when occasionally put to me directly — "Can I have your name?" — always puts me in a tricky position. On the one hand, I am, in general, not great at accepting help, even more so when it involves taking up space in people's minds, hearts, and prayers. On the other hand, refusing such a request/offer is certainly rude and ungrateful, not to mention a lost opportunity. Of course, I always reply in the positive, and usually even give my real name. But I often add, if not to maintain the functional mechanics of *tefillah*, then at least for myself, that I would appreciate if the prayers' prayers would be somewhat specific. The natural contestant—to be cured—involves an outcome that in principle may be possible, but would be considered, all things considered, in defiance of nature, and I'd prefer to save my miracle credits, nonexistent as they probably are, for another occasion. I ask instead that if anyone is so inclined to daven for me, it should be a more realistic *tefillah*: that my relapses will be few and far between, that the periods of treatment will be bearable to the extent possible, and that during the remissions I will function maximally. I'm aware that this is still a lot to ask, but it's far less miraculous, the lesser of two kindnesses.

The real quandary, however—"The Davening Dilemma"—awaits at the other end of the journey: when to stop? With a "traditional" illness, one that officially has a point that can be defined as a full recovery, there is, at least in principle, a clear time at which it is logical and appropriate to stop davening for the *refuah* that has already been granted. Perhaps, even when dealing with a condition that may return at some future time, at least in the meantime the subject can be considered fully healthy, with a history of illness and the potential of history repeating itself. But what happens when the condition is chronic, and it's just a matter of time before it is once again active? I am a past patient, and a future patient, but am I a patient in the present? Is my state continuous? This is a perfectly simple, albeit tense, question. And does it make a difference if the patient is receiving maintenance treatment or no treatment at all? Even the most detailed *hilchos tefillah sefarim* don't appear to offer much in terms of definitive answers to these questions.

An extra complication is that, in general, asking people to stop davening for a *choleh* can have two very different, indeed opposite, connotations. Let's just say that if someone blesses you that you should be removed from the *cholim* list, it's probably best not to answer *Amen*, at least not without first asking for clarification.

The matter of complete recovery, or lack of potential thereof, also raises a question that probably bothers only the most pedantic of pedants: use of the phrase *"refuah sheleimah."* How do you respond to such a blessing, knowing that it is highly unlikely to come true? Obviously, the answer is politely, with sincere appreciation, and with the traditional *Amen* or thank you. But, in theory, should the blessing be downgraded to "You should have some level of incomplete *refuah* within the boundaries of what can realistically be considered a good result for a *nebach* in your condition"? That certainly deserves an *Amen*, but I'm not sure I would give it a thank you.

Then there's the matter of learning for someone's *refuah*. Here, for reasons I may or may not fully understand, I feel much more comfortable with the gesture. I think that a significant factor is that learning with someone in mind is much less personal than davening for someone. *Tefillah* is such an intimate encounter with God, and having someone insert your name and well-being into their prayers feels invasive. Learning, on the other hand, is learning. The experience itself isn't necessarily altered by the added intention, and if my health can piggyback on someone else's good fortune of having an opportunity to learn, I'm more than happy to come along for the ride. Besides, I've dedicated my entire working life to teaching Torah. If, by my mere existence (or threat of its absence), more Torah is learned, in a sense I'm still promoting *talmud Torah*. The fact that it takes place without my involvement, leaving me more time to engage in "fruitful" activities, such as these musings, needn't bother me. I'm fully aware that this distinction probably says more about me than about these two invaluable activities. Perhaps helping me gain clarity on this matter is something people should have in mind when they learn for me.

There is, nevertheless, one aspect of learning for someone's benefit that did bother me at one point, and that is the association, at least in my mind, with the most common form of learning for someone, namely, to merit a deceased. Soon after I was diagnosed, I found out that two of my close and dear *talmidim* had initiated a large scale learning project for my *refuah*. They named it "*Torat Emet*," a nice play on words, though naturally not exactly a titanic task considering that my name does make it quite easy to come up with titles for books, learning projects, and Gerrer Rebbes. Deeply touched and ill at ease as ever, I was uncomfortable when I found out about this. Mainly because I misunderstood the nature of the initiative. The web page featured a picture of me, a brief description of the situation, and an email address for contact. My immediate impression was, "Great, now people are signing up to learn Mishnayos in my memory."

This, however, was just me jumping to conclusions. Upon inquiry, I found out that it was something else altogether. One of my *talmidim*, a young and exceptional *talmid chacham*, was sending out daily emails containing halachic essays spanning a wide variety of topics to the people who enlisted. This went on for five hundred consecutive weekday installments, and by the end there were several hundred recipients, including friends, students, students' friends, friends' students, and a significant number of perfect strangers.

It appeared that my concern—that the learning project had the appearance of a still-alive *sheloshim* sign-up sheet—was in vain. Or so I thought, until I made the one-time mistake of checking the comments section of the page. There I found the following message written by someone I didn't know or had ever heard of: "*Yasher koach* on this great initiative, I really enjoy the emails. *Purim sameiach* to the family. May the learning be an *iluy neshamah* for the *niftar*."

Needless to say, I was quite shaken when I read this, though probably not as shaken as he was when I replied.

Life truly has something new for us every day. You live and learn.

42
Fishing for Complements

Looking for an alternative to conventional medicine? Have you tried "dying"?

Dr. Hertz, Pain Clinic Director

I deeply distrust any statement that starts with the words "Four out of five doctors recommend."

The Fifth Doctor

Throughout the duration of my first bout with cancer, which lasted fifteen months, I treated the side effects of my treatment with traditional medicine: painkillers for the pain, anti-nausea medication for the nausea, and sleeping pills for the insomnia. These means were effective on quite varied levels: the painkillers were quite effective, the anti-nausea medication was quite useless, and the sleeping pills were at first quite effective and later absolutely useless.

I didn't go out of my way to find alternative ways to alleviate my symptoms. ("Symptoms," for those unfamiliar with the official medical term, is an elegant cover word for any and all forms of suffering that you experience as a result of anything in life.) My approach was to trust the doctors. They have experience treating patients and are familiar with tested ways of best helping them, I told myself. I still believe this, and I have no grievances with them. But through my experiences I have learned that the doctors' main focus is treating the cancer, with the patient's general well-being in mind as a major consideration, while the patient would be well-advised to focus on his general well-being, with the cancer in mind as a major consideration. I have no problem with this, it's totally legitimate. Divide and conquer: you kill the cancer; I'll try to stay alive long enough to enjoy your success.

Perhaps the sense of novelty that accompanied the first experience contributed to my somewhat passive attitude toward seeking relief. In round two, my mindset was completely different. As they say, "Been there, done that, got the trauma." My approach changed radically from "If it isn't offered, I probably don't need it" to "If it exists, I'll find it and try it." As a (very low-ranking) veteran, this time the division of labor was clear to me from the start: their job is to attack me with pills and needles; my job is to do anything possible to counter everything they do to me. This time, pills for the pains and pails for the nausea wouldn't do. I needed an alternative.

The first thing I did was look up the definition of "alternative medicine" to see what I was up against. What I found is something very interesting: dictionaries and encyclopedias have opinions. Compare, for example, the following five definitions, arranged in a particular order:

- "The treatment, alleviation, or prevention of disease by such techniques as...allied with attention to such factors as diet and emotional stability, which can affect a person's well-being" (*Collins English Dictionary*). Subtext: "Totally legitimate. Could help." A fairly positive view.
- "A range of treatments for medical conditions that people use instead of or with Western medicine" (*Cambridge English Dictionary*). Subtext: "Not included in the undefined category of 'Western medicine.'" Pretty meaningless. Perhaps a bit condescending toward the East.
- "Any of various systems of healing or treating disease not included in the traditional medical curricula of the U.S. and Britain" (*Merriam-Webster*). Subtext: "Not on the list." Still somewhat meaningless. A bit condescending toward Europe and the rest of the West.

- "Any type of treatment that does not use the usual scientific methods of Western medicine" (*Oxford Learner's Dictionary*). Subtext: "We have our methods, and we think they are better." A distinct whiff of superiority.
- "Any practice which aims to achieve the healing effects of medicine, but which lacks biological plausibility" (Wikipedia). Subtext: "A bunch of rubbish." A full-blown put-down.

My attitude toward all of this was that all the definitions were, by definition, wrong, or at best useless, on two accounts. First, these were all definitions by negation, describing what alternative medicine isn't. Granted, since the term is "*alternative* medicine," the definition will inevitably be formulated in such a manner, but at the end of the day, it's about as useful as defining a category of shapes that aren't a hexagon. It tells us very little, or to be accurate, only one thing, about them. Second, and as a natural result of the first problem, this negative category lumps together a multitude of practices that have little, if anything, essential in common. As such, it surely stands to reason that they should not be seen as a concept, and certainly should not be treated equally. Introducing minerals into your digestive system should not be in the same category as waving them over your body, and being treated on a massage bed probably contributes more to your well-being than rearranging its position in your house for better energy flow.

In the spirit of negative definitions, the question of which forms of alternative medicine *not* to engage in seemed quite clear. The question of which to try out was less so. I approached a local center for alternative medicine, where a doctor (ironic, I thought) recommended a combination of three forms of treatment: acupuncture, tuina massage, and reflexology. I didn't ask for clarification and assumed that he meant one at a time rather than having needles rubbed into the soles of my feet, though I wouldn't be surprised if someone somewhere did offer such a service.

The problem with such experiences is, of course, how to assess their effect. I wasn't necessarily bothered with the scientific aspect of lacking empirical evidence of their legitimacy; the dictionaries had that covered.

I was concerned with the practical question of which treatments to persist with and for how long. After all, these treatments are not only an alternative to conventional medicine; they are also an alternative to holding on to your money.

So, I came up with a brilliant plan. I would approach it methodically. I would try out each treatment separately for a period of six weeks and record the results. Between each two types I would have a control period of no treatment. This way I would be able to observe and isolate the effects of each of the therapies. Then I remembered that I needed relief sooner than half a year later. That considered, I gave up on my genius plan and just delved into the full combination. Having too many alternatives simply left me with no alternative.

My impressions of the treatments were varied. In some cases, I left the sessions feeling quite good, while at other times I was in a bad way. This seemed to depend mainly on how I felt prior to the sessions. Still, I managed to garner some insight about the various therapies and their impact on my well-being:

Regarding the tuina massage, I can't say I'm convinced that cancer can be cured by the vigorous digging of an elbow into one's calf, but I did find the experience deeply enjoyable, and the results were tangible and immediate. The only significant drawback was that after each session I had to vacate the table, which was a real challenge since by that point my muscles had all the rigidity of a soft gel. I suggested to the practitioner that as an extra service, he should provide a bed onto which the massage client is spilled after the treatment. This would benefit not only the parlor patron but the institute, too, as they could easily pull the old "cinema popcorn move" and charge more for the lodging than the treatment itself, and in all honesty, it would be worth it.

The masseur whose services I employed was a charming fellow who gave all the impression of being professional, and indeed, within a few minutes my muscles felt relaxed. That is, except for one particular group of muscles, which appeared to be getting a proper workout: my mouth muscles. His technique seemed to involve engaging the client in constant conversation, a practice that may be enjoyable to some, but for me personally is a burden, whether within a massage situation or any circumstance for that matter. I imagine that it would have been entirely acceptable to request that he give me the silent treatment, but as so often is the case, I decided to just take it lying down.

One particular session ended with the massage therapist offering me some gourmet chocolates that he happened to have brought with him, making the impossible claim that he had "eaten too many already." Though I didn't know him very well, I figured I could hardly regard this as taking sweets from a stranger, considering the fact that we had engaged in long conversations and experienced more physical contact than I would be comfortable with even with my closest acquaintances. Plus, he offered me some gourmet chocolates, so there wasn't really much of a dilemma.

Acupuncture was certainly an interesting experience. Of the three therapies, this was surely the hardest for me to evaluate, and by hardest I mean probably impossible (in my case). Without a doubt, it was, if nothing else, a relaxing experience, as it involved a bed and a quiet, darkened room, generally speaking a good recipe for some well-needed tranquility. Although, the relaxation was somewhat diminished by my constant worry about what to do if the needles fell out. I wasn't sure what the proper etiquette was in such an occurrence. Upon sharing my prickly concern, the puncturer told me about a client she once treated who, instead of calling for help, had indeed taken matters into her own hands, or to be accurate into her own face, and shoved a fallen needle into a random place on her forehead. It would be great to end this story with the surprise reveal that she accidentally discovered the cure for migraines, but, as far as I'm aware, all she discovered was an ineffective cure for embarrassment.

Reflexology, which has already featured earlier in my story, turned out to be an enjoyable and, I believe, effective treatment. It appears that in the five years that passed since my hospital pedal encounter, my discomfort level had not lessened, but nonetheless the experience had a noticeable effect, both during and after the session. This was somewhat ruined by the necessity of then having to walk on my freshly tenderized feet, and in this case, I had trouble coming up with a strategy that would solve the problem. Asking for a piggyback or slithering home would probably have been quite an effective way of preserving my feet, but somewhat detrimental to my dignity in the former, and every other part of my body in the latter. Lacking any good solutions, I had no choice but to walk, trampling all over the good work that had been done.

After completing an initial set of treatments over a period of several months, and experimenting with one other, juicy therapy, I decided to stop. (I also visited a chiropractor, which I believe belongs in a different category altogether. I was quite tickled, though, when the first one I contacted said, without a trace of humor, that he was abroad but would be happy to treat me remotely. Granted, in our post-COVID world, Zoom sessions aren't unusual, but I think that aligning my spine virtually is taking things too far.) I didn't feel that I was benefiting enough to justify continuing. Of course, I couldn't rule out the possibility that without the treatment I would have felt worse, or that more time was needed for the effects to become noticeable. But neither would I ever be able to confirm these possibilities.

All in all, it was mostly an enjoyable experience, within the narrow boundaries of enjoying anything related to treating the horrendous side effects of a serious illness. But at some point, all good things, and bad things, and things indeterminably good or bad, must come to an end.

In conclusion, I'm all for alternative medicine. As long, of course, as it's not used as an alternative to medicine.

43
Respiratory Respite

Intoxicating inhalants, such as nitrous oxide, are no laughing matter.

Dr. Al Dante, D.D.S.

The question isn't so much if coffee is a drug, but if unproductiveness is an illness.

Z.Z. Napsalot

Disclaimer for minors: this chapter contains disappointing content.

We're quite far into my ill odyssey and the pages of this book, and I imagine that some readers, at some point, have found themselves wondering, "So, is he going to talk about cannabis, or not?" After much deliberation, I'm unequivocally impartial to announce that the answer is yes, he is. But if a chapter about medical marijuana is something you are excited about, be warned: you may be deeply disappointed. He certainly was.

Whether legal or not (which depends on where you live), whether it *should* be legal or not (which depends on how you live), and whether it's God's wonder or the Devil's poison (which depends mostly on the word "medical" being inserted in front of it), there comes a time in one's career as a patient suffering from an illness of some degree of seriousness when one faces the delicate dilemma: should one turn to the option, ever increasing in popularity, of using medical cannabis for relief from a variety of ailments? Be it the symptoms of the illness itself or the side effects of its treatment, many swear by it, and not only dealers (or, as they are known these days, "pharmacists"). Some patients may even secretly delight in the opportunity to engage in such an activity in a legal, justified, and socially acceptable manner, and experience the recreational aspects. Others don't bother with the secrecy.

I myself had lived a very sheltered life and had no experience of such activities, not even by proximity. As such, I was very hesitant to consider the possibility, and didn't make any inquiries into the procedure of obtaining a license or research the potential benefits and harms of herbal remedies. Only deep into round two, after coming to the realization that suffering with dignity involved much more suffering than dignity, did I decide to be open to the suggestion, which I promptly made to my doctor. It turned out that he wasn't a massive fan of the idea, which probably explains why he had never brought it up. "If you really think that a few puffs of something will make everything better," he said, "that's just a pipe dream." His lack of support notwithstanding, he gave me a prescription, together with a disclaimer that I might end up in the emergency room. I wasn't sure if this was a formal warning, an informal invitation, or both. I reluctantly accepted the former and politely declined the latter.

As a non-smoker, I opted to start with oil. This attempt was short-lived, however, as my gradual progression achieved anything but gradual results. Increasing the dose slowly, a few days at a time, I experienced the following: one drop—nothing; two drops—nothing; three drops—nothing; four drops—BOOM. For the first time in a long time, I was pain free. In theory, success. The problem was that, in addition to feeling no pain, I also lost all other forms of feeling and was practically paralyzed for twenty-four hours, trapped in my own body, hardly able to move, somehow still managing the short zombified journey from my bed to the fridge and back every few hours for a semiconscious snack. That was the end of that experiment.

Traumatized by the event, I abandoned the idea for several months, but after being told repeatedly that my mistake was using the oil form instead of smoking, I decided to give it another go. Having no experience with firsthand smoking, I found the experience very unpleasant (a factor you probably don't consider when you choose a non-smoking lifestyle), but I persisted in the name of the good cause. Unfortunately, this method, too, didn't appear to bring about any significant results, unless we consider coughing fits and a burning sensation in the back of my throat a result. I figured that, without any benefit, introducing more toxins to my already highly toxified body was probably not a great idea, and I abandoned this course of action, too.

My final attempt at consuming the wonder drug was via the third and allegedly best method—vaporizing. Recommendation for this way of using the product came from two very different sources. The first was a pharmacist, who explained that this was the healthiest, best-controlled, and most efficient way to absorb the substance. She clarified that she herself had no experience with any form of marijuana use, medical or otherwise, but was communicating what was reported by many customers. The second recommendation came from a much more experienced, albeit less professional, professor. Having pretty much given up on the whole endeavor, I chanced one day upon an all-things-smoking-related shop, and on a whim decided to pop in for an impromptu consultation. I had a suspicion that the young man behind the counter was a consumer himself. I deduced this from some subtle clues, chief among them the fact that he was at the time actively engaged in consuming a large portion of the shop's stock, puffing away every few seconds on a small handheld vaporizer he kept perched on the counter. This ventilating veteran, who once fought enemy fire with fire and was currently similarly fighting his military PTSD with PTSD (perpetually taking serious drugs), was a slick salesperson if ever there was one (and there probably was). Ten minutes later, I left the shop with the exact same model, after completing a short course in vaporizer operation and maintenance and a quick review of the various strains of cannabis and their respective recommended uses. I opted to pass on the optional session about how to make your own high-quality oil.

I was excited about this new and promising prospect of a relatively odorless, inconspicuous, and unharmful method of treating my pain, fatigue, and insomnia. But, once again, I was to face disappointment. Aside from some mild tingling in my legs, a meager increase in appetite, and the inability to focus on anything, I experienced no substantial effect, and my high hopes went up in smoke. The pain, fatigue, and insomnia persisted. The only thing I was relieved of was a considerable sum of money.

As is often the case in life, if you're waiting for a magic cure, don't hold your breath.

44
Long Time No See

Eagles have incredible eyesight; they can spot a book at two miles, swoop down, and catch it in motion. A pointless exercise, considering their poor reading skills.

To Mock a Killing Bird, 2020

"Most patients cope relatively well with the impaired vision caused by the treatment," said the ophthalmologist. "You can be optimistic."

I responded to this statement with an appropriate moment of silence, assuming mutual recognition and therefore not bothering to note the unintended pun. It was, at least in my eyes, too obvious, and as such, funnier to let it go unmentioned. I fear, however, that perhaps this unsaid pearl of punnage went unappreciated, as it is entirely possible that he was more focused on the substantive content of our conversation than potential distractions in the form of wordplay. To compensate for this lost opportunity, my vision for this chapter is to not spare the reader the myriad of potential sight-related puns, hopefully without losing sight of the main goal of the chapter. With that in mind let's move on, or, more accurately, go back to the beginning.

In order to qualify for the clinical trial, I had to tick a few boxes, in addition to the many boxes I had to tick when filling out the application form. (Permission to use your DNA for further research? Sure. Let me know when my clone arrives, I have a list of jobs as long as his arm.) One of the main conditions for joining was the condition of my eyes, as they would likely be the main victim of the treatment.

An assortment of various forms of misery and suffering, more commonly referred to by the official and misleadingly mild name "side effects," is part and parcel of any cancer treatment. For each treatment, the question is not "if," but "which." Pick your poison, literally. Mostly, the side effects aren't particularly surprising. Hair loss and nausea certainly win the prize for being the most featured in popular media. Stomach cramps, fatigue, insomnia, and mood swings, albeit somewhat less famous, are familiar, too, at least to the initiated. But sometimes treatment throws you a curveball, which is very tricky to catch (or bat, or avoid, or whatever it is that's taking place in this sports analogy) when you can't see, which would be the case with this particular trial drug.

One might wonder exactly why and how a treatment aimed at battling malignant cells in the bone marrow would affect a patient's eyesight, and indeed one did wonder. My attitude throughout my medical saga has been one of only mild interest in the science behind the illness and the treatment, with my main interest lying in staying alive. But in my layman's understanding, the general idea is something like this: traditional chemotherapy attacks all fast-splitting cells, which unfortunately include not only cancer cells, but anything related to the digestive system and hair. In an attempt to minimize the side effects, "antibody drug conjugates" have been developed, in which the chemotherapy drug is linked to an antibody drug that is specific to the type of cancer being targeted. What (hopefully) happens is that the drug finds the cancer cells and releases the medicine directly into them, as opposed to uninvitedly invading every part of the body with utter disregard to common decency, thus (hopefully) sparing healthy cells from exposure to the chemotherapy and minimizing the side effects of the treatment. Hopefully.

On paper this sounds amazing. After all, if you really must wage war against yourself, you're probably better off using a guided missile than a bomb.[1] But life is seldom lived on paper; reality tends to present us with hardship and hazards. Life is less about paper and more about rock

---

[1] This analogy should not be seen as professional military advice. Before shooting a guided missile or detonating a bomb, always consult your local weapons expert.

and scissors. (Shoot.) As is the case with many treatments, fixing or attempting to fix one problem often comes at the price of creating another, essentially swapping a cow for a donkey, which, although not great, may ultimately be the better option, as donkeys are less detrimental to the environment. In this particular case, the cost of living was enduring lesions to the corneas, resulting in blurry vision.

To assess my compatibility with the treatment, I had a preliminary meeting with the ophthalmologist supervising the clinical trial at my hospital. After conducting the necessary examinations and finding that I did indeed qualify for the trial (i.e., that my eyes were in good enough shape to be assaulted), it was time for the briefing. This consisted primarily of preparing me for the multitude of eye-related side effects that I was to expect over the course of the trial.

"First and foremost," declared the doctor, "the most common and almost certain side effect is dry eyes. You'll have to apply 'artificial tears' every few hours." "Artificial tears? That won't be necessary," my wife retorted. "We have more than enough authentic ones." I had difficulty reading his reaction to this humorous (and honest) reply, since he didn't provide one. But as they say, absence of confirmation of a joke isn't confirmation of a joke's absence, so I chose to interpret his silence as speechless awe.

"In second place," continued the clinician, "a slightly upgraded version of the first option, namely the sensation of having sand in your eyes."

"The what of what in my what?" I exclaimed, wondering if I had experienced a brief blackout during which we had, for some inexplicable reason, changed the topic from treatment to torture. "You know that extremely uncomfortable feeling of irritation you get when there's something in your eye, let's say an eyelash or an airborne speck of something or another?" he said. "Well, that sort of feeling, but covering the entire surface of your eyes and without the possibility of relief, since removing nonexistent sand is infinitely harder than removing the regular kind. The best you can do is use eyedrops for this, too." I guess the assumption is that if you absolutely must have sand in your eyes, it should at least be wet sand. "And by the way," he added casually, "stay away from wind and air-conditioning. They tend to increase the irritation." Wonderful. Wet, hot sand.

"Lagging behind in third place," said the surgeon, "though this is less common, there might be some inflammation."

"Oh, that's just swell."

"Also forthcoming," spelled out the specialist, "you might suffer from photophobia."

"Already have it," I said. "Hate having my picture taken."

"And finally," proclaimed the practitioner, "the biggest challenge, if indeed it does transpire, is impaired vision. Corneal ulcers begin to form on the outer perimeter of the eyes, and with time they spiral inward until they start obstructing vision. The lesions won't be visible, but then again, neither will much else for you at that point. This is fully reversible but will likely last for the entire duration of the treatment. It's important to keep in mind that throughout this time you won't be able to drive." Great. As if it wasn't bad enough that I didn't have a car, now I wouldn't even see well enough to not drive.

"In summation, it won't be a stroll in the park for you, mainly because if you attempted that, you would probably walk into a tree. But we'll make sure to see you through it. And generally speaking, my view is that it is through our struggles that we find true meaning in life," philosophized the physician. (I should clarify, there was only one doctor present. He was just multi-roling.) I didn't particularly appreciate this insightful nugget; perhaps I was already starting to experience trouble with depth perception.

I had, of course, been warned about this possible infliction as the main potential cost of the experimental treatment. Indeed, this was pretty much the only real cause for deliberation, since otherwise the treatment offered greater success and milder side effects.

Terrifying and debilitating outcome notwithstanding, I had already decided to take the plunge. Opting out was a tempting but shortsighted choice. If things become too hard to handle, I reasoned, I could always drop out. Generally speaking, not a particularly admirable approach to commitments, but appropriate under the circumstances, I believed.

We commenced the treatment, which comprised the experimental drug in addition to two traditional ones. Within no time at all, the classic side effects kicked in, as did the dryness in the eyes, but signs of negative impact on my vision were nowhere to be seen. I was tempted to declare myself a certified member of the fortunate few club, those statistic-defying individuals who had endured the treatment without affliction, but I realized that to sincerely adopt such a belief would be both naive and unwise. As they say, "Expect the worst, hope for the best, and embrace cognitive dissonance."

And then one day, about two months into the trial, I suddenly realized that I couldn't read. Two thoughts immediately sprung to my mind: (1) I really should have paid more attention at school. (2) Disappointment isn't a massive fan of proportionality. Even with my most reserved and minimal degree of optimism, the letdown was immense.

The drug finally lived down to its reputation, and the effect was fast and severe. The decrease in visual acuity was so extreme that, according to the clinical trial protocol, we had to put the treatment on hold until there was some improvement, as well as lower the dosage from that point on for the duration of the trial. In fact, on my following semi-weekly visit to the clinic, in addition to not receiving the trial drug due to the damage to my eyes, I also wasn't given the standard drugs thanks to stomach issues. Sitting there that day, looking up at the plain bag of fluids I was hooked up to, I thought to myself, "In today's experiment, ladies and gentlemen, we are going to find out if saline can cure cancer." Talk about pouring salt on a wound.

Thus began a period of ten months of impaired vision. A lot happened during that time, but it was all kind of a blur. The basic schedule consisted of an excruciatingly long visit to the eye clinic every third week (with treatment twice a week during the first two) to get the OK, or not OK, to receive the next round of treatment. Eighteen visits in total, not including the visits in which I arrived, as per my appointment, only to find that the one doctor who was authorized to oversee my case was absent, which was both highly frustrating and not particularly great for my health, as it interrupted the treatment schedule. On the subject of clerical mishaps, one time, during a strike at the hospital in which only limited services were available, the eye clinic canceled all non-life-threatening-related visits, essentially keeping open only their version of an intensive care unit, which, disappointingly, is not officially referred to as the "I-don't-C-U." The mass cancellation included my upcoming appointment, and it was of little, if any, comfort to know that someone, or more likely, an automatic messaging system, was feeling positive about my prognosis. My assumption, which proved to be correct, was that this was an oversight; it was easy to see how this could happen—there was simply a lack of coordination in the eye department. After explaining the situation to the receptionist, who contacted the doctor for confirmation, my appointment was uncanceled.

In addition to all the foretold side effects, I experienced a bonus eye-related affliction that wasn't even on the list: a succession of styes. (If you don't know what that is—first of all, consider yourself fortunate; secondly, don't google it on a full stomach, it's not a pretty sight.) There's only so much a hot compress/tea bag/boiled egg can do for you, and at the end of the day you're stuck with a sore, inflamed eyelid and a less-than-attractive lump on the eyelash line. Aside from being painful, it was another contribution toward obstructing my vision, as in some cases my puffy eyelid forced my eye halfway shut. Interestingly, the ophthalmologist insisted time and time again that this was in no way related to the treatment. This was hard for me to believe, going on both statistics and logic. Statistically, I had in the past experienced perhaps four styes over the course of as many decades, and now suddenly I had one every few weeks. Logically, we were messing with my eyes, and something was going wrong with my eyes. My theory is that we were both right. He was correct that the styes weren't caused by the medication, since styes result from a blockage in the oil gland of an eyelid, and there's no correlation between that and whatever havoc the chemicals were wreaking inside my eyes. But I'm confident that this was no coincidence, and my running assumption is that the constant application of eyedrops and rubbing my eyes to alleviate itchiness played a major part. Basically, rather than being a side effect of the treatment, it was a side effect of the treatment of a side effect of the treatment. This distinction was of little help, though; pedantry isn't much of a painkiller. Fortunately, home remedies for styes abound. A quick Google search yielded fruitful results and I was excited to find a web page dedicated to treating this particular affliction. It was a site for sore eyes.

It's hard to describe clearly just how frustrating it is not to be able to read properly, so I'll describe it blurrily: Like so many things in life, it's hard, if not impossible, to fully appreciate something until it's gone or somewhat diminished. This is certainly true regarding clear vision, which we rely on, without thinking twice, in almost every daily activity. What was most frustrating for me was the inability to read or learn. But the difficulty extended far beyond that and included such routine necessities as reading text on a phone, typing on a computer, identifying bus numbers, and many such tasks. An illuminated magnifying glass was helpful for some reading activities, though not very comfortable for extended periods and not a particularly great look in public.

Coping with limited vision was no simple undertaking when it came to teaching. Throughout the treatment period I managed to maintain my teaching responsibilities for most of the academic year. In addition to the general challenge of functioning while often not feeling great, not being able to read posed a direct obstacle. I did much of the teaching off memory, though some minimal preparation was possible if I held my notes right up to my face, once again, not a great look. Helping students read sources was close to impossible, and the closest I got to being fully useful with that aspect of the job was occasionally learning with students in the adjacent park in which the natural sunlight was slightly better for my poor vision than its artificial counterpart.

One thing I learned during the many eye examinations was the magical property of the pinhole effect. The first stage of every examination involved holding up the traditional occlude, a "device" (flat piece of plastic with a handle) that covers one eye while testing the other. After looking through the regular hole, a pinhole attachment would be swiveled down to cover the hole and the test would be repeated. Not the broadest view, but the effect was startling, truly a case of seeing is believing. The previously blurry, vague, faded shapes on the screen were suddenly transformed into crisp, clear numbers. This was an eye-opening moment for me, and immediately got me thinking about finding a way to implement this simple technology in my everyday life. Was the solution to my troubles hiding in plain sight all along? Had I overlooked the obvious?

My first idea was quite unimaginative: to get hold of an occlude of my own, though this would not be particularly convenient and only effective for one eye at a time. My next big idea was to find some sort of pin-holed, lens-shaped surface to affix to my glasses somehow. I ordered what I thought was exactly that online, but when the paper-thin package arrived it turned out to be stickers that one is meant to apply to glasses for use in a shooting range. Admittedly, it's entirely possible that my diminished eyesight was partially to blame for the blunder. I can't say I fully (or even remotely) understand the purpose of this product, not the least since they appeared to almost completely obscure vision, and, considering that I would have made a poor marksman at that moment in time, I didn't bother looking into it. Next, I tried to fashion a clumsy makeshift version by cutting a small hole in a piece of sturdy craft paper, but the result was less than unsatisfactory. As the months went by and the list of failed attempts grew longer, my desperation reached unprecedented heights. The whole process culminated in what must have simultaneously been one of the funniest and most pitiful scenes in this saga, as my wife entered our living room one day, only to find me sitting in an armchair, book in hand, and a perforated spatula pressed against my face. It was time to admit defeat.

As the year came to an end, I had a final meeting with the ophthalmologist in which the tone of the conversation was somewhat more casual than usual. Looking back at the difficult year I had experienced and wanting to highlight just how challenging my impaired eyesight was, I told the story of my unsuccessful efforts to achieve pinhole success, all the way to its ridiculous kitchenware conclusion. "Oh," he said, "you could have just used 'pinhole glasses.'"

"Pinhole glasses?" I responded, bepuzzled.

"Pinhole glasses," he repeated. "I once had a patient come in with them. He had a prescription, but for some reason he refused to wear glasses.

Instead, he had a pair of solid black plastic glasses with pinholes across the entire surface of what would otherwise be the lenses (available at AliExpress for $0.33, discount coupons available). Strange, but he swore by them."

I guess hindsight really is 20/20.

45
Read between the Lines

This isn't going to be as bad as you think. It's going to be much, much worse.

No Doctor Ever

My frequent visits to the eye clinic—eighteen in total—involved not only seeing an ophthalmologist, but also regularly having my vision thoroughly tested by an optometrist, thus accumulating more such visits in the span of a single year than many respectable bespectacled individuals do in a lifetime.

Much to the benefit of everyone involved, these appointments took place almost exclusively with the same optometrist, with only one exception, details of which to follow. It's hard to find an accurate word to describe the type of relationship that develops under such circumstances, since "acquaintance" seems too cold, while "friendship" sounds too warm. Be the Goldilocks term what it may, we certainly developed a basic familiarity, greeted each other warmly upon meeting every three weeks, and conversed comfortably and jokingly during our many sessions. (Granted, the setting lent itself to a relatively narrow band of relevant joke material, with little or no variation from visit to visit, but that didn't stop me.)

Due to the regularity, frequency, and uniformity of the visits, the procedure quickly became routine, and little, if any, instruction or prompting was necessary. Right eye; right eye with pinholes; left eye; left eye with pinholes; red half or green half? Top line; second line; third line; smaller and smaller letters; chin here, menacing machine with bright red light;

seemingly endless variations of "And what about this? Better with, or without? This is with, this is without. One, or two?"

But it wasn't always exactly the same. On one particular visit, I arrived only to find a substitute optometrist. A creature of habit and habitual worry, I was unsettled by this change of routine (a concern that, incidentally, turned out to be justified, as I had to return to repeat some of the tests that weren't recorded according to the very specific requirements of the trial guidelines, adding extra time to what was already a half-day event). Upon politely inquiring as to the whereabouts of my regular practitioner, I was informed that he had taken off a few weeks due to his recent marriage, a life decision that, apparently, he did not see fit to run by me for approval. Ever forgiving and eager to express my sincere congratulations, I decided to surprise him on my next visit with a personalized greeting card.

I had something quite specific in mind, but, considering the abundance of novelty items and niche-filling specialty products one comes across these days, I was still surprised to find that I couldn't find it anywhere online. It appeared that even those card manufacturers boasting the most diverse content hadn't anticipated this particular situation. As a result, I resorted to making it myself, which gave it a personal touch, specifically the sloppy touch of a five-year-old's art project.

It was a pretty simple design. The outer sleeve was a standard card. Inside, at the top of the first page, appeared the words "Mazal Tov" in big letters. The second line read "Mazal Tov" in slightly smaller letters, and so on and so forth, until the letters were no more than a series of tiny dots. The opposite page read, "Which is better: with, or without? One, or two?"

He was amused and deeply moved by the gesture, which I assured him was done with full sincerity and out of the kindness of my heart, sentiments that I was committed to maintain on the strict condition that he refrain from making any additional major life choices until my clinical trial was completed.

Having my "own" optometrist, and having such frequent visits with him, produced not only creative gifts, but, more importantly, more accurate test results. Our familiarity, once gained, contributed significantly toward reducing one of the more counterproductive behaviors many of us tend to employ: not being entirely straightforward during an eye examination. If there's one test in life where it's most definitely not in your best interest to pass without merit, it's an eye test. As it is, stretching truths and bluffing are not usually particularly commendable. But they are at least, at times, understandable. Cheating yourself out of the pair of glasses you need, on the other hand, is just plain silly. And still, many of us find the experience highly stressful, as if the goal is to correctly identify the numbers on the screen, rather than the numbers of our prescription. Are we ashamed of our imperfect eyesight, or are we just naturally driven to perform well and be successful, or at least appear so, regardless of the immediate and long-lasting ramifications? Do we somehow feel as though we're letting the optometrist down by not managing to read his numbers, and do we really think that giving ourselves a little edge by leaning forward and squinting is a good idea, considering that by doing so we are sentencing ourselves to a life in which we can only see properly by employing this method?

It starts off nice and easy: lovely, sharp numbers. The difference between right and wrong is very clear at this point, and the rule is simple: say what you see. A few clicks later and the lines start getting blurry. Be it an oversight or by clever design, the font they use isn't particularly helpful—the eight and nine are almost identical. Soon you start taking chances: if it looks like either, you choose one at random and end on a question mark, unless you've already identified one of them elsewhere in the line, in which case you select the other by process of elimination. At some point further down the lines, the betting stats become slightly harder to compute, as the six enters the equation, too. You follow similar but slightly modified rules for the other numbers. At a later and more advanced stage, all you see is five dots, but you still go strong with the guessing game. Ultimately, it culminates with the examiner interrupting your meaningless number-blurting ramble to inform you that the display isn't even on anymore.

"Better with, or without? One, or two?" innocuous a question as it may seem, is possibly the most stressful of them all, as there is almost always virtually no difference between the two options, and if there is, it involves two different variations of blurriness that are impossible to classify as being better or worse than each other. On top of that, you are put on the spot and given hardly any time at all to make this all-important choice, time that you waste trying to decide which blurry digit is almost clear enough to use as a marker for this riddle. You get two free tries, but even then, you're not ready to commit, fearing the dire consequences of this judgment, so you ask to see each again, knowing full well that seeing it one or one hundred more times won't make the slightest difference. Self-conscious of having selected the "they're pretty much the same" option too many times running, you take a chance and choose a side, desperately hoping that he doesn't sneakily check again later to test for inconsistency.

I'm certain that I'm not alone in experiencing this, though I imagine I've had the chance to develop a more methodical system of self-sabotage than most, given the sheer number of my consecutive examinations. A further complication was introduced when I realized that it was very hard to even determine, for the benefit of my subconscious, which outcome was more desirable—passing or failing. Each three-week treatment cycle was preceded by an examination, and treatment could only be administered if the results were satisfactory. "Satisfactory" translated loosely into "the degree of damage caused by the previous cycle was insufficient to force a stop according to the trial protocol." With a "good" result, I could go ahead and receive treatment. With a bad result, I would have to skip the following cycle. In my eyes, neither option was particularly great. It wasn't so much a case of good and bad, but bad and worse, and it wasn't at all clear which was which. Treatment meant a win for the trial, and ultimately, hopefully, my long-term well-being, but three weeks of misery for me. No treatment meant a win for cancer, giving it more time to progress, but a short break for me, with a chance of some improvement in eyesight quality, albeit fleeting. As such, it was hard to feel enthusiastic about either outcome. If there was any real winner in all of this, it certainly didn't feel like it was me.

The reason for the rigid testing routine was the known negative effect the trial drug had on the corneas, causing a significant percent of participants to experience significantly blurred vision. Statistics, as we know, are a complex matter, and it takes a trained professional to properly analyze and apply them. One thing, however, is "clear" to all: statistics are very useful for predicting what will happen. To other people. But surely not to us. After all, we're special, not just a statistic like all other regular people. The fact that the statistics comprise people who all believe the exact same thing, nullifying the possible truth of that already empty belief, doesn't stop us from secretly hoping to defy the odds. I probably wouldn't admit to it at the time and risk tarnishing my reputation as a realist (aka pessimist in denial), but I certainly harbored a fantasy of undergoing the treatment entirely unscathed.

As it turned out, I was indeed special and didn't fall within the norm. Unfortunately, I deviated from the mean in the less desirable direction. I experienced severe blurriness for the most part of ten months. At its worst, I couldn't recognize faces from a distance of a few feet, giving the impression that I was being rude and ignoring people I knew when crossing paths (or, from a different perspective, finally having an excuse to do so). At its best, I couldn't read, leading to me going stark raving mad from boredom and frustration.

Though I was warned about this possible effect, neither the doctors nor I expected it to be as extreme. My situation was far worse than the one other patient in the clinic who was receiving the same treatment, whose surname, frustratingly, was "Sees," an observation I shared repeatedly with anyone interested, and plenty who weren't, including Mr. Sees himself. ("So-and-so Sees," I would quip, "but I don't.")

There must be a simple solution, one would imagine. Blurry vision, after all, is what glasses are for. So all I needed to do, in theory, was get new glasses. In theory, as they say, there's no difference between theory and practice. In practice, there is. I could indeed buy new glasses to match my new prescription. The problem was that I would have to do this every day, as my prescription was changing, continually and dramatically, in no particular and consistent direction. At first, the ophthalmologist was sure that the optometrist was incompetent, or at least making some serious mistakes in his examinations or recordings of the results. But unfortunately (for me, and fortunately for the optometrist), there was no mistake, other than me agreeing to join the clinical trial in the first place, perhaps.

Halfway through the year, I came up with an idea that might at least offer some improvement: calculating the average of all the different prescriptions of the past ten visits and getting a new pair of glasses that at every given moment would at least be better than my currently useless ones. In my mind, this was a great plan, but apparently that's not how eyes/prescriptions/glasses/optometrists/averages work.

There was, in fact, one "simple" solution to this conundrum all along: borrowing the optometrist's testing kit—the clunky adaptable empty frame and the full case of lenses that slot into it and putting together a new pair of glasses every day. That would be quite a spectacle. The reasons why this idea didn't materialize are numerous, varied, and quite unnecessary to name, as is often the case with ideas that are simultaneously ingenious and ridiculous. But the truth is that even if such a plan or one similar to it was feasible, it wouldn't have helped all that much, since even with the corrected prescription my vision wasn't that great.

And so, I had no choice but to accept my new reality. Reading and writing were out. Most computer and phone use were out, too. I was assured that the situation was temporary and would pass when we ceased treatment (or about two months thereafter, as it turned out), so there was light at the end of the tunnel. But that didn't help much, since it, too, was out of focus, and it certainly didn't illuminate the tunnel itself.

As a sighted person, with a routine prescription low enough for me to sometimes not even notice when I forget to put on my glasses, I'm not in a position to complain and wallow in misery about a relatively short period of time in which my vision was restricted. Plenty of others have it worse than me, permanently. The message of this chapter is not "behold the *nebach*." The lesson is that sometimes in life you have to lose one thing before you can find another. I had lost the ability to see properly, but little did I know that this would lead to me learning how to listen. By this I don't mean something biological, like gaining a sharpened sense of hearing in compensation for my diminished sense of sight and developing echolocation. That would be batty. Nor do I mean something deep like an increased sense of social acuity and the ability to really "hear" the other. I mean something much less dramatic but much more exciting: I learned how to listen to podcasts.

Up until that point, I knew only two things about podcasts: that they existed, and that I had no inclination whatsoever to engage with them or find out more about them. Here was a vast audio world of easily accessible, portable, valuable content to which I was totally oblivious. It was there all along, hiding in plain sight, as a result of my plain sight. In an instant, my constant boredom and frustration were replaced with readily available, practically infinite options of learning and entertainment. In particular, this was a precious opportunity to explore subjects that I had not had a chance, or the resources, to study before. My knowledge of Jewish history and prominent figures within it has since increased tenfold. My already keen interest in and great appreciation of Biblical, Rabbinic, and modern Hebrew has grown. And fifty episodes into a series on the history of the English language have brought me ever-so-slightly closer to understanding why any connection between spelling and pronunciation appears coincidental.

They say that you don't know what you have until it's gone. But you also don't know what you don't have until something else is gone. For me it was one thing; for each of us it could be something else.

By now, thank God, my vision has been fully restored, and those challenging times are something I look back at with great relief. But the treasures I picked up along the way, including the daily quality time I spend with my daughter listening to entertaining, kid-friendly science podcasts at bedtime, are still present. They are indeed something to look forward to.

POSTSCRIPT—VISIBLY SHAKEN

On a final optical note, there was actually one pleasant sight surprise waiting for me at the end of the trial. In the final eye examination, it transpired that after all the erratic changes in my prescription, when things finally settled down, my eyesight in one eye was slightly better than it was to begin with. This made no actual difference to my life, not the least since monocles aren't exactly high fashion these days, but I thought it was both interesting and amusing. My suggestion, however, that this course of treatment be used in lieu of laser eye surgery, was deemed neither.

46
Man's Search for Gleaning

One who chases laughter, laughter runs away from him.

Citation not needed

At some point, one has to wonder, do I now observe all medical experiences through the prism of "How do I find this funny for the book?" Do I artificially inject humor into mundane situations, graft amusement onto dire circumstances, or at least keep an eye open for future anecdotes?

During my first round of sickness and treatment, this wasn't a factor, since at the time I had no intention whatsoever of writing anything. The idea to do so occurred and developed organically only some years later. During round two, I was certainly conscious of the possible prospect of putting things in writing.

The answer, however, is a resounding "There's just no need." Life does a good enough job of providing the potential for humor all by itself. The only help it needs from us is an openness to see the occasional ripples of comedy in the otherwise roaring seas of adversity.

I will admit, however, to one case in which I actively "searched" for entertaining tidbits in real time. This was, in fact, the final hospital visit related to my most recent saga. Perhaps this played a part in creating my mindset, and I was somewhat conscious that it would be a while, hopefully, before I next had the opportunity to find new material.

The numerous eye styes in my little eyes had eventually healed and left no visible marks. All but one, that is. Long after discontinuing my treatment, right in the center of my left upper eyelid remained a lump, approximately the size of a lump. Even after being partially drained by means of what I hope was an official medical procedure in which the doctor squeezed it between two cotton buds (yes, it was as painful as it sounds), a decent-sized bulge remained. Over the course of the following weeks, it waxed and waned, but always remained. Uncomfortable, obstructive, and not particularly easy on the eye.

After much mulling and musing, I decided to take up the ophthalmologist's offer to remove it, despite his use of the phrase "dig it out."

When the day came, I checked myself into the hospital and began the process of preparing for the procedure. As can only be anticipated, there were unexpected complications. Fortunately, they were clerical, not medical. At the reception counter of the ward, we were told that we had the wrong papers. (This common phenomenon, I gather, is a result of a sophisticated system in which one's bag is scanned upon entering the building, and an algorithm is activated that identifies the one vaguely relevant but essential document that you don't have with you.) In an attempt to amend this error, we paid a visit to the office that produces the papers and were given the right papers, which were still the wrong papers. After bouncing between the two offices a couple of times, the two receptionists discovered a smart little invention called "the telephone" and managed to sort things out, and we got to move on to the next level.

In this challenge we had to deal with the matter of the blood-clotting disorder that I had contracted back in chapter 1. As a "safety measure" (to not bleed to death), prior to any "invasive procedures" (mind your own business, procedures!) I need to receive medication that "promotes blood clotting" (join thousands of satisfied customers and try blood clotting today!). So far this had been applied only to bone marrow biopsies, and this was the first time I was undergoing a procedure outside my home court, the hematology ward. As a result, there was much uncertainty regarding the preparation for the puncturing: which drug to use, what dose to give, how long in advance, and why didn't this patient come with a user manual. In retrospect, perhaps this was my responsibility, but it was my first time, so I'm willing to forgive myself. Fortunately, the nurses in the ward were slightly more technologically advanced than their receptionist counterparts and had already discovered the wonders of the telephone, and were thus able, not entirely without delay, to locate the proper authorities and attain the required information.

By this point we were several hours behind schedule, or, as measured in "hospital time," right on schedule, and it was hard to say that I found any of this particularly funny. Obviously, that's how it was going to be; the one time I was actually on the lookout, there was nothing to see.

Then it was time to get dressed for the occasion, and I was given the full garb: a hospital gown and disposable surgical head and shoe covers. It felt very overdone, having a full wardrobe makeover just for a tiny incision in my eyelid, but I guess that's the procedure for such procedures.

Finally, about six hours after arrival, I found myself sitting outside the operating room, waiting to be called in. The surgeon came out to call me in. He took one look at me and said, "Are you sure you want to have this procedure? There's nothing there."

Well, perhaps "nothing" was a slight exaggeration, but indeed the lump was significantly smaller than it had been two days earlier when we'd met and decided to go ahead with the surgery. It was small enough that the bruising, swelling, stitching, and possible scarring would most likely be worse than the affliction they would be replacing. Apparently, in some cases, having an appointment with a dentist can actually cure the cause of a toothache, not just repress the sensation of pain in order to avoid dealing with it.

I'm not sure exactly which aspect of this I found funny, but I did. Confusing, surreal, and funny. I think part of it was realizing how strange it was that at no point between admission and moments before surgery did anyone involved take a look and comment, "Hmm?" And part of it was just the quick succession of the two sharp transitions, from hours of dull waiting to the intensity of sitting outside the operation room in full garb to being dressed, packed, and on my way home within minutes.

One way or another, it so transpired that at the one moment when I was least expecting it, I found something amusing, or at least bemusing, once again learning that "one who runs away from laughter, laughter will run after him."

Our senses don't create sights, sounds, and smells; they just enable us to perceive them. The sense of humor is no different.[1] Only a fool would deny that life serves us a hefty portion of challenges, pain, and hardships. But it would be foolish to deny ourselves some laughter, especially when it presents itself to us on a silver-lined platter.

---

[1] In anticipation of the torrent of comments to surely follow from the physics/philosophy buffs who will argue that sights and sounds are indeed a product of our senses, since without our subjective perception they are merely waves (or particles, or both), I will gladly concur, but claim that my analogy still stands. If a joke tells itself in a forest and nobody hears, it isn't funny. I will also point out that this isn't a science book, though it remains unclear exactly what kind of book it actually is.

47

The Writing on the Wall

Never bring a pen to a sword fight.

S.T.M. Schreiber

We all know the stories: man breaks leg, checks mezuzos, finds a problem with the words "*u'v'lechtecha va'derech.*" Man injures hand, checks mezuzos, finds a problem with the words "*al yadecha.*" Man has serious heart disease, checks mezuzos, finds a problem with the words "*al levavecha.*" Man has severe eye condition, checks mezuzos, finds a problem with the words "*bein einecha.*" Man has trouble falling asleep, checks mezuzos, finds that the word "*u'v'shachbecha*" is missing, or that the *sofer* has written "*u'v'shachbecha u'v'shachbecha.*"

Or perhaps this: man loses credit card, checks bank statement, finds out that someone finally booked the luxury holiday he's been dreaming of for years, checks mezuzos, and finds a problem with the words "*u'v'chol me'odecha.*" Man sleeps through alarm in the morning, checks mezuzos, finds a problem with "*u'v'kumecha.*" Man has trouble with self-control in regard to baked goods, checks mezuzos, and discovers that "*v'achalta*" is written with a big *aleph* and "*v'savata*" with a small *sin*. (He doesn't bother fixing this; every diet allows for the occasional small sin, he reasons.)

There are some unknown stories, too: man breaks leg, checks mezuzos, they're fine. He doesn't tell anyone about it, silently joining tens of thousands of other leg-breakers with kosher mezuzos. Man doesn't break leg, checks mezuzos, finds a problem with the words "*u'v'lechtecha va'derech*," doesn't know if to be relieved or disappointed, and where exactly he fits in this whole discussion.

Like many things, mezuzah checking and interpreting is a fascinating subject. Like many things, it's not a simple concept to understand, specifically the precise "mechanics" at work. (Is the *pasul* mezuzah the cause of the affliction or just an indication to it? If it's a cause, why would such a mistake, made by someone else, merit such a punishment? If it's a sign that something is wrong and something needs to be done, why hint to the infliction, of which the inflicted is already fully aware, and not hint to the key to the solution? "Man breaks leg, checks mezuzos, finds a problem with '*u'v'chol me'odecha*,' gives tzedakah, and recovers successfully" could be a great story, but undeniably lacks the same panache.) Like many things, the subject is subject to hot debate. But most importantly, like many, many things, it's a subject regarding which I have limited expertise, and by limited I mean none. I have no expertise, but what I do have is the following interesting experience.

A few years ago, somewhere between part one and part two of my story, for reasons entirely unrelated to my condition or any other condition other than wanting to have kosher mezuzos, we employed the services of a local mezuzah checker. After inspecting our mezuzos, it transpired that two of them were *pasul*. Both contained the same mistake. The issue was the first word of the last *pasuk*, the word "*l'maan*" in "*l'maan yirbu yemeichem*."[1]

"What does this mean?" my wife asked the mezuzah man worriedly. "It means," he responded, "that you need new mezuzos."

Curious to know if there was a correlation in timing between the mezuzah mishap and my recent adventures, I asked the *sofer* if there was any way to vaguely approximate when they became *pasul*. "Actually," he responded, "I can tell you the exact moment they became *pasul*."

---

1   Specifically, in both cases, there was a problem with the *ayin*. At the time, this detail seemed insignificant. In hindsight this is quite intriguing, considering that my future attempts at extending my days on earth would feature "a problem with the *ayin*," times two.

"Wow, you're good," I said. Just how good was soon revealed when I inspected the handiwork of the scroll he wrote specially for me—his invoice.

It turned out that the mezuzos were *pasul* from day one, or to be accurate, they were never kosher. The problem with the letters was part of the original writing, not a result of fading or peeling or any other possible later occurrence. This complicated things further. Now, in addition to the basic question of what, if anything, we make of such a thing, there was also the added question of who we make it for. The original owner had bought and put up the faulty mezuzos, and subsequently lived in the apartment for twenty years. Then I came along and inherited them (the mezuzos). If I were inclined to believe that there was a message here, I would perhaps be selfishly inclined to believe that it wasn't intended for me, a mere newcomer arriving on the scene. But did that mean that there was a bad omen looming over the heads of the previous owners, and if so, was it my responsibility to contact them and advise them not to invest too much in unripe avocados?

As a rule, I tend to be quite skeptical. To maintain a healthy balance, however, I make a point of also being skeptical about skepticism, and therefore I still don't know exactly how I feel about this issue, both as a general concept and regarding my personal experience. What do we make of this? What does it all mean?

There might only be one way to resolve this. One day, when reading stories of mezuzah wonders, we might come across the ultimate tale:

"Man has doubt regarding the validity of mezuzah messages, checks mezuzos, finds that all his mezuzos are *pasul*. In all cases, almost the entire text has completely faded. Remaining are only the words '*v'hayu…l'os…mezuzos beisecha*.' Man sues *sofer*."

48
Wait Watchers

You never get a second chance to make a second impression.

Mark O'Hammer

The shortest distance between two points cuts straight through the line.

B.A. Skipper

Now that I've been through the cancer-and-treatment experience twice, a question I'm occasionally asked, mainly by myself, is if the second time is different from the first. The answer I usually give is that there are plenty of differences. Some are a function of age and physical condition, some depend on the nature of the treatment, and some are just a matter of being desensitized to certain aspects of life as a patient, for better or worse. An example of the latter category is the following.

Throughout my first stint as a card-carrying disability-card carrier, I used my exemption from standing in line only once. Thereafter, I didn't feel comfortable taking advantage of this license to thrill. This was mostly, I told myself unconvincingly, due to moral considerations. No one likes waiting in line, and so long as I was physically able to endure this universal trial, I felt it was the proper thing to do. It may have also been, just a tiny bit, in order to avoid the evil glares of fellow queuers. But it was mainly the moral thingy.

This noble approach, however, didn't last forever. To my credit, it lasted for quite some time, several years, in fact. But that's a lot less than forever. The transitional moment took place after my relapse, on a visit to the post office to collect what was probably going to be a disappointing letter about an eternal mortgage rather than an exciting package. I wasn't feeling amazing (about the prospect of waiting in line for an hour, which was a regular occurrence), and I decided to finally take advantage of my queue-cutting privileges. It was then that I discovered, not without embarrassment, that they didn't exist. The clerk took a quick look at my card and pointed out that at the bottom, in small writing, it only said, "Free admission for accompanier," and not "Exemption from waiting in line." This was not in accordance with the letter that had accompanied the card upon its arrival, but that historical tidbit didn't seem to impress her.

On discovering this deflating information, I mused over two philosophical quandaries: First, would I still receive reward in heaven for all the past times I'd refrained from using the card now that it turned out I didn't actually have such rights after all? Second, I puzzled over the logic behind this distinction. If, according to "them," I was incapable of spending a relaxing day at the zoo without the physical and/or emotional support of a caregiver, how in the world was I expected to stand in line for ages to get into the zoo in the first place?

Quite soon after this discovery, I happened to find out, by pure chance, that the law had just been changed, and from now on I was indeed exempt from queuing. Now, I'm not saying I wanted payback, but let's just say that in the months that followed I angered some impatient people in post offices and pharmacies and made an above-average number of visits to museums and zoos, granting free entrance to my daughter (who accompanied me to the latter as compensation for the former). At the zoo, as a nice little bonus, I also made use of a mobility vehicle, and to be honest, the whole experience was not so much a visit to a zoo but rather a go-kart race through narrow, windy paths against a backdrop of sleepy animal scenery.

One slightly awkward queue-cutting moment took place in the post office, where I seemed to be spending a curiously significant amount of time, which is quite ironic considering that the whole point was to spend less time there. While not-waiting in line, I glanced at my card and noticed that the expiration date was in a few days (I was using a new card that had arrived after the rules had changed, not my prized old one with a six-hundred-year expiration date). As I stepped forward, a displeased bystander made some comment, to which I responded that my situation was hardly one to invoke jealousy since my special rights were due to me having cancer. I then added that I didn't have much time left anyway, just a few days, in fact. She was much more understanding after this little misunderstanding.

All things considered, though, I think my use of the (literal and metaphorical) cancer card has been within the boundaries of good taste, and my queue skipping hasn't been out of line. Others have been observed stretching the boundaries a little. I once witnessed a man trying to cut the line to see a nurse on account of his cancer. This might have been acceptable enough if it weren't for the fact that it took place in the waiting room of an oncology outpatient clinic.

I shouldn't judge, though. At the time, I was on round one, and as far as I know he might have been on round one hundred. Considering the decline of my own inclination to stand in line after just two rounds, by the time I find myself in his place I'll probably be doing the same, if not worse, and at some point, if I make it there after 120, I'll probably try and pull off the ultimate move and cut the line to heaven. Who knows? I guess I'll just have to wait and see.

49
Two Strikes and You're In

The bad news is that you have cancer. The good news is that we have the bad news.

Doctor Allflesh

Cancerversery [noun]—a term I coined to refer to the date of my diagnosis but soon stopped using because people were wishing me many happy returns.

The Complete Dictionary of Incomplete Truths

When I was diagnosed with cancer, I thought that was pretty bad news. When I was told it was chronic and would recur, I thought that was pretty bad news, too. When I found out that it indeed had recurred, I thought that wasn't such great news, either. But it turned out that the most heart-sinking news was yet to come.

When, after a five-year break, we resumed treatment, I joined a clinical trial that consisted of nine cycles of three weeks each, amounting to approximately six and a half months. When those were concluded, I learned that this was only phase one of the trial, in which I received the trial drug in addition to two other, traditional drugs, and that there was a phase two, which involved the trial drug alone, and was open-ended. This was definitely not what I had been expecting or hoping for, but I figured I could manage it for a while longer until my condition was stable enough to move on to phase three, which was hopefully phase "now I'm free." Moreover, I comforted myself with what I assumed to be a logical deduction—that the side effects of one drug would surely be fewer in number, lesser in intensity, and overall easier to deal with than those of three.

As it turned out, in this apparently simple calculation I was very wrong, since one of the drugs that was discontinued was a steroid that had the redeeming quality of keeping me from being in a constant state of absolute exhaustion at all times. Perhaps kids have a point when they complain about learning math and ask when they'll ever use it in life. If something as basic as 3 − 2 = 1 doesn't hold true, what hope is there for Cartesian geometry, holomorphic functional calculus, and other such branches of mathematics that show up when you google "complicated fields of mathematics with fancy names I've never heard of"? And let's be honest, "inconsistent mathematics," "fuzzy mathematics," "pointless topology," and "Lie algebra theory" do very little to boost the trust appeal of the discipline as a whole.

Four miserable months later, I met with my doctor to discuss several issues, most importantly (to me) the unspoken looming matter of what the future held. Leaving the least desirable for last, I finally asked what my expectations should be in terms of the future, namely round three of the illness. That's when I received the news that in my eyes eclipsed all previous bad news in its badness. There wasn't going to be a third round.

No, I wasn't dying. Nor was I, by means of some miracle, cured. There wasn't going to be a round three because, apparently, round two was scheduled to continue "forever." He explained that once myeloma makes a comeback, we don't really expect it to do a go-away, and therefore the standard procedure is to try and keep it at bay by treating it continuously. Forever. Well, as forever as humanly possible. As far as I was concerned, there must have been a misunderstanding. (This wouldn't be the first time I misunderstood a doctor. Consider the following absolutely true interaction, recorded verbatim: Me: "I was recently bitten by a dog; should I be concerned about rabies?" Doctor: "Where were you bitten?" Me: "In Yerushalayim." Had this been intended as a humorous response, or a weak attempt at one, I would be moderately proud of myself. It was, however, a sincere answer, and as such I'm more worried than pleased with myself.) Until that moment, I had been under the impression that my life plan was a series of "wash, lather, repeat," or "recover, relapse, re-treat," in ever-repeating cycles—an already dismal prospect, but one that suddenly seemed highly attractive in comparison.

As a rule, I don't doubt my doctor's expertise. Indeed, I once shared with him that, much like Austrian zoologist Konrad Lorenz's newly hatched ducklings, who imprinted on him and waddled after him around his village, I saw him as a mother duck of sorts, and in principle would follow his counsel regarding all cancer-related matters. But just in case he had momentarily gone absolutely mad, I triple-checked with two other doctors in the clinic, and it turned out that, as it happens, he had in fact not lost his mind. A life sentence of treatment was indeed the standard procedure, considering my current situation. And what about having to deal with the horrendous side effects indefinitely? In response to that query, one doctor put it to me succinctly and bluntly. It came down to a simple choice: quality of life, or life. Well, when you put it that way...

Naturally, this was not exactly amazing news (unless, of course, we consider the actual meaning of the word amazing: "extremely surprising"). It was bad enough to find out that I was going to be in treatment for the foreseeable future. Worse still was the fact that the treatment I was undergoing at the time was what you could call "great for the cancer but awful for the patient" (technically awful for the cancer, too, if we consider the cancer's point of view), as it had the nasty side effect of causing lesions to my corneas, resulting in blurry vision, and rendering me unable to read. A foreseeable, unseeing future. There was the option of switching to a different course of treatment, but the medical team's strong recommendation was to stick with it since there was no guarantee that one of the alternative options would be as effective. I agonized over this choice between two bad options and wished I didn't have to make it.

With such decisions it's very hard to know where to turn for guidance. The doctors, who know as much as there is to know, are able to lay out the options and tell you that they can't tell you what to do. Conversely, some people you encounter, while knowing absolutely nothing about the options, are still somehow "able" to tell you what to do. Most people are equipped with neither ability. At the end of the day, no matter how much support you have, when it comes to making a choice, you're on your own.

In the end, my wish was granted, and I didn't really have to make a choice at all. A very decisive agent intervened and made it for me. Kidneys are described by Chazal as giving counsel—*"klayos yo'atzos"*—and mine didn't disappoint. Or, if one were inclined to adopt a negative perspective, they did disappoint, big time, as they suddenly appeared to forget how to absorb protein. The medical team was puzzled by this development, as it had not been observed in any of the other patients participating in the trial worldwide. A group of nephrologists assembled to discuss the matter and presented me with three possible explanations: the first possibility was that the kidneys were misfunctioning as a result of the illness itself. This seemed unlikely, however, since the relevant indicators showed that at this point the treatment had been quite successful at repressing it. The second possibility was that the problem was a result of an unrelated kidney disease. The doctors believed that this was highly unlikely and too big a coincidence to be considered a legitimate possibility. What are the chances that you have two rare, unrelated conditions, they said. My wife's cynical but sincere response to their rhetorical question was, "You clearly don't know us," but this quip didn't seem to affect their medical opinion. The third possibility was that the problem was a side effect of the treatment. This, too, seemed unlikely, since, as mentioned, no such reaction had previously been documented.

After further investigation into the limited literature available, it was revealed that the phenomenon had indeed been observed in subjects of this particular trial drug. It just so happens that they weren't particularly human. I was curious as to what exact species my fellow sufferers belonged to, and what became of them, but that information wasn't available, at least to me.

I wasn't sure exactly how I felt about this development. Was it fair that this information was withheld from us (human) participants? The papers I signed upon admission to the clinical trial detailed the known side effects and how commonly they occur. Included were findings such as "X percent of patients experienced fatigue," "Y percent suffered from nausea," and "Z percent reported blurry vision" (by the way, to save you the bother of turning to the back of the book for the answers, and contrary to the statistics provided in the forms: X=Y=Z=100). Nowhere did it mention that "W percent of mice involved in the experiment suffered from kidney damage." Perhaps the subjects hadn't signed an interspecies medical confidentiality waiver. Did they at least share this finding with the other mice before injecting them with the drug (or the cancer)?

I don't know if having this knowledge in advance would have impacted my decision to join the trial, but it was definitely about to be a consideration for quitting it, as it was now the most likely, in the sense of "least unlikely," explanation for my kidney problem.

To test this theory, we ceased treatment, and indeed, after a few weeks the kidney function slightly improved. To test the test, we resumed treatment, and indeed, after a few weeks the kidney function proved the theory to be right. The readings were still low enough to resume treatment according to the trial protocol, said the pharmaceutical company running the trial, but high enough for it to not be in my best interest, said anyone who wanted me to live. We decided to stop treatment. But where did that leave me? I needed to be in treatment, but the best option was no longer an option.

Once again, it turns out that life defies mathematics. Two negatives, added to each other, traditionally result in a larger negative. It stands to reason that bad + bad = worse. But reason only gets you so far in life. The current treatment, harsh as it was on the patient, was even harsher on the illness. The cancer readings were lower than they had been in years, indeed lower than at any point since my original diagnosis. And so, it was decided to temporarily break with standard procedure and take a break from all treatment.

Life is often very much a matter of perspective. Under the right conditions, and viewed from the correct point of view, even the words "You're going to have to start treatment again one day" can be considered good news.

50
Love of Labor

Boredom [noun] — a bleak condition contracted by children and cured by having them.

The Complete Dictionary of Incomplete Truths

Take the night shift, and you'll never have to work a day in your life.

Oved Laylah

The timing of my relapse was such that I was able to finish the academic year and commence treatment once the summer break began. As a teacher, this was the ideal time to receive treatment (to the extent that we can describe something like this as ideal). There were many benefits to this scheduling:

1. For once, I would finally have a ready answer to the pre- and post-summer-break questions, "Any plans for the summer?" and "Did you do anything interesting this summer?"
2. I would be able to keep the interference with work to a minimum.
3. The early stages of the treatment, in which my body would be adjusting, would take place during a time when I had very few responsibilities and could afford maximum rest.
4. I would have ample time to experiment with various forms of pain/nausea/fatigue/mood relief and management, traditional or otherwise, and find the optimal medication/diet/routine/

transcendental meditation regime (to the extent that we can describe something like this as optimal).
5. I could use the summer months as a gauge to assess how functional I was while in treatment and how realistic it would be for me to work during the following academic year.

It didn't take long for the treatment to start taking its toll. To be precise, it took about one day. One could argue that this was a blessing of sorts (to the extent that we can describe, etc.) since it extended the period of time in which I could conduct my experiments and make my assessments. I would, however, not recommend putting forward this argument to friends or loved ones who might be undergoing a similar experience, at least not if you wish to remain friends and loved. Thank God, I had my wife by my side to take on much of the heavy lifting and enable me to rest.

That also lasted about one day. On the first day of my treatment, we found out that she had mono (technically making us sick in stereo), a condition primarily known for causing extreme fatigue. As far as being sick and tired, we were, literally, in it together. Needless to say, however, despite her condition she did indeed take charge of the many responsibilities that fell to her, mainly because she's amazing, and also because in the "rock, paper, scissors" of "cancer, mono, and any other illness," cancer beats mono and the other illness, the latter two battle it out for second and third place, and the process has no resemblance whatsoever to "rock, paper, scissors."

As the summer weeks went by and the data rolled in, five things became abundantly clear:

1. I was much less excited about using my newfound response to the post-summer activities inquiry, and in that vein, I was glad I had decided to spare my colleagues the awkwardness and hadn't used it in response to the pre-summer one.
2. See number 5.
3. The naive hope that the adjustment period would have any upper limit or exist at all was soon dispelled, as the reverse seemed to

be the case, with my physical condition worsening week by week, probably due to the accumulation of toxins in my body or some other equally unhelpful explanation.
4. Despite my best and varied attempts, I hadn't found a way to manage the side effects efficiently.
5. Judging by my current state of (dys)functionality, maintaining a regular work schedule would pose quite a challenge.

With all these considerations, and my general well-being in mind, my wife was strongly opposed to the prospect of me resuming work in the upcoming school year, at least in full capacity.

As a rule (issued by my wife), I rarely overrule her verdicts. To do so would be both foolish and perilous. But this was one decree to which I could not concede. There was no question that she was absolutely right—what my body needed was rest. But my soul needed something else. It needed purpose and it needed to be occupied. And it needed those things not only for itself, but for the body it was inhabiting, too. And this purpose and occupation was to be found in teaching.

When I originally decided which profession to pursue, there were three major factors I considered: self-fulfillment, contribution to others, and financial security. I chose teaching, reasoning that two out of three ain't bad. What I didn't realize at the time, but later came to appreciate, cherish dearly, and try to live up to, is that teaching isn't just a profession—it's something much more fundamental.

I like illustrating this realization with the following story. I was once at a family *simchah* and found myself sitting at a table beside a stranger. We got talking, and one of the first things I asked, as one does, was "What do you do?"

"I work as an accountant," he responded. "You'll notice," he continued, "that I didn't say 'I'm an accountant.' That's not what *I am*, my essence. What *I am* is a Yid. What I *work as* is an accountant." He seemed quite proud of this insightful bit of wit, and rightfully so, since this was a lovely and inspiring attitude toward life and self. He then proceeded to ask what I do for a living. "I'm a teacher," I responded. "You'll notice," I continued, "that I didn't say 'I work as a teacher.' Teaching isn't just my profession; it's part of my essence. I teach, therefore I am, a teacher."

Another thing I find in teaching is a sense of constant renewal. This may sound strange to those who haven't experienced it, considering that in most teaching situations there is a set curriculum, and the subject matter is on a repeat cycle. The astronomer Clifford Stoll said, "The first time you do something, it's science. The second time, it's engineering. The third time, it's just being a technician." That may be true in science, but in teaching, if you're fortunate enough to be teaching the right thing to the right students, every time you do it it's both science and art, and nothing can be more interesting, fresh, and exciting than that.

Of course, when teaching Torah, there are additional aspects of value. When outlining the mitzvah of *ahavas Hashem*, the *Rambam* writes that the mitzvah also includes calling other people to His service and belief in Him. Just as when you love a person, he explains, you praise him elaborately and call on others to love him, so too when you love Hashem, you do what you can to help others reach that same state. This is also true regarding Torah. When you love it, you want to share that love with other people and help them appreciate and love it, too.

So, there really wasn't much of a dilemma. For me, that is. As long as I was physically capable of teaching on a level that I believed to be satisfactory, providing my students with the full learning experience they deserved, that's what I would do.

And that's what I did.

It required a slightly liberal approach to painkiller consumption, some opioid patches, a bit of steroids, more painkillers, and some creative napping solutions for coffee-resistant midday exhaustion, but I did it.

I made it till Purim. Then it was time for *v'nahafoch hu*. I had done all I could to control my enemy, and now it was time to accept that, for the time being, my enemy was going to control me. (I am referring, of course, to the illness, not my wife.) At least partially. We compromised, and subsequently I took the mornings off. The completist in me really wanted to tough it out for the two remaining weeks of the *z'man*, but by that point it wasn't really a matter of choice. I simply wasn't physically capable of teaching on a level that I believed to be satisfactory and providing my students with the full learning experience they deserved. In fact, during the morning hours, I wasn't physically capable of teaching at all, or much else for that matter.

Challenging as it was, I don't regret this episode, and I believe that the good far outweighed the bad, both for myself and all other parties involved. If nothing else, one good thing that certainly came out of the whole experience was just how amazing the following year was in comparison, helping me appreciate, not for the first time, that normal is the new great.

Would I do it again? I probably would, and I probably will. It seems that I may have been too busy delivering lessons to learn one myself. But who knows, perhaps with (more) age will come wisdom, if not true wisdom, then at least enough sense to realize that my wife knows best.

There's a time for *mesirus nefesh*, and a time for *shemiras ha'nefesh*. Figuring out when to cultivate a *nefesh chayah* and when to tend to a *nefesh ayeifah* requires serious *cheshbon ha'nefesh* and can easily lead to *agmas nefesh*. Ultimately, *v'nafshi yodaas me'od*—you just know—it's not something you can teach.

51

(Not) The Final Chapter

Every rule has an exception, including this one, and the rule of three.

Exceptional Quotes, vol. 2

The big question is, what now? And the answer is very simple: I don't have a clue.

Essentially, life goes on as normal, punctuated by a series of tests every three months (these are in addition to the special tests I request sporadically to see if we can find any signs of hypochondria). As I write these very lines, I'm waiting for the results of my most recent blood tests, in which one little (or not so little) number will determine if tomorrow will be just another day, or the first day of a new round of treatment, with all the misery and uncertainty that accompany it.

I won't pretend that this aspect of my life is fun or funny, or at least I currently can't think of a way to make it so. If anyone has any ideas, I'm open to suggestions. To be honest, my coping strategy is to follow the only piece of advice I find useful in this type of situation: "Don't think about it."

I won't go as far as saying that I feel as though I'm living on borrowed time, but there is definitely, on some level, the sense that I don't have full ownership over it, and that at some point it's going to be snatched from me, perhaps not completely, but at least in terms of the freedom to use it as I choose.

I ended part one of this book with a lighthearted reference to the high likelihood of a part two. I don't want to repeat myself here, just as I don't want the events to repeat themselves. But deciding how to close is proving difficult. A deep and witty one-liner would be ideal. But nothing about this is ideal, which I'm totally fine with, so I'm equally fine with forgoing a perfect sign-off.

A story is meant to have a beginning, a middle, and an end. But this story is far from over, and as coauthor of my own life, I plan on writing as long a middle as possible, so I'll just leave things open for now. Will there be a part three? Who knows? Not even my doctor. Even if there is, it still won't be the final chapter, just another middle, perhaps followed by yet another middle, and as many middles as life prescribes me.

The truth is that it isn't even really the middle, because every day is a new beginning, with a 100 percent chance of new possibilities, new opportunities, and new excitements. What more can I ask for?

Acknowledgments

This book has been made possible thanks to the dedication of family, friends, and students, all of whom are the source of true happiness.

To my soulmate, Nechama, and the six precious souls we've been blessed with. If not for you, this would be a very different, and very short, book; it would read: "Life is unbearable. The End."

About the Author

After sufficiently absorbing British culture and humor, Rabbi Yonatan Emmett, aged six, moved to Israel to pursue more noble goals. He later attended Yeshivat Sha'alvim, where, over the course of eighteen years, he learned, served in the IDF, received *semichah* from the Chief Rabbinate of Israel, and taught. Prior to this book, Rabbi Emmett published a more traditional *sefer*, *Aliba D'Emet—Sugyot Yesod B'Hilchot Berachot* (Mossad Harav Kook, 2018). Presently, Rabbi Emmett divides his time between teaching at Michlelet Mevaseret Yerushalayim (MMY), editing classic Torah works for the Shlomo Aumann Institute, and trying to write this paragraph.

He lives.

In loving memory of

David Stern

June 18, 1937–Aug. 17, 2021

Caring husband, loving father and grandfather, adored uncle

Dedicated by Helena Stern

In loving memory of

David Berg

Feb. 20, 1940–April 26, 2021

A wise, gentle, and loving family man

Dedicated by Barbara, Miriam, and Beverly

In loving memory of

Gila Landman

June 4, 1945–Oct. 9, 2015

Loving wife, mother, and *savta*
A poet and a dedicated teacher

Dedicated by Reuven Landman

In loving memory of

Ruth Rice

May 22, 1935–Oct. 21, 1995

A true *eishes chayil*, exemplary mother, and beloved sister
Descended from greatness, greatness she imparted

Dedicated by the Rice family

In loving memory of

Barbara Goldsmith

Jan. 18, 1963–Nov. 18, 2014

A mother with unmatched dedication to her children and a sharp sense of humor—that even Rav Yonatan would appreciate

Dedicated by Maury and Atara Goldsmith

In loving memory of

Sharon Shenker

May 12, 1977–Jan. 23, 2023

A loving wife, dedicated mother, and respected mentor
A powerful presence sorely missed

Dedicated by the Shenker family

In loving memory of

Danielle Grajower

Oct. 15, 1985–Oct. 27, 2018

A beloved mother, wife, daughter, and sister

Dedicated by Micah and Becky Epstein

In loving memory of

Bryna Greenberg

June 17, 1999—Jan. 25, 2022

Cherished daughter, beloved sister, kindhearted friend,
and devoted student, who enjoyed and appreciated this book
in sickness and health

Dedicated by the Greenberg family

L'iluy nishmas our fathers

ישעיה נתן בן מאיר פרייליך ז"ל
בנימין עקיבא בן שלמה שטיינבאק ז"ל

In their *zechus*, may our children be blessed with good health,
mazal, and berachah, as they journey through life doing
mitzvos with a smile

Dedicated by Eitan and Gabriella Freilich